Training Excellence

A Comprehensive Guide to creating and delivering Exceptional Training Courses

Jimmy Miller MA, Chartered MCIPD

Contents

Praise and Recognition
Repetition is the mother of all learning
Working the group
How to deal with reluctant learners
Closing the course

Communication
Rapport
Getting the message across
The Arc of distortion
Verbal Communication
Non-verbal Communication

Level 1 Evaluation
Level 2 Evaluation
Level 3 Evaluation
Level 4 Evaluation

Using Visual Aids
PowerPoint
Handouts

How to remember names
Mind Accessing
Mind Accessing Stories and Anecdotes
Mind Accessing Attention grabbers
Icebreakers and introductions
Exercises
Quotations

INTRODUCTION

Why I decided to write this book

Why training courses fail

About the author

Jimmy Miller is a learning development specialist with over twenty years' development experience. Founder and Managing Director of his own successful Training Company, Jimmy has a Master's degree in Strategic Human Resource specialising in learning and development, a Human Resources degree and is a Chartered Member of the Chartered Institute of Personnel and Development.

Jimmy had a successful sales and management career working in Retail Banking, Finance and Insurance and the Motor Industry. He received accolades and rewards culminating in the award for United Dominions Trust Salesman of the Year. United Dominions Trust was one of the UK's largest Financial Institutions.

After working in managerial and developmental roles Jimmy displayed a natural aptitude for training. In the training environment Jimmy found himself to be a "round peg in a round hole" and embarked on his learning and development career in 1997.

Jimmy attended many "train the trainer" residential training courses which helped expand and reinforce his training abilities and stimulated a thirst for academic success to mirror his increasing experience. Whilst providing training facilities in the financial sector from Human Resource training to Management Development then providing Sales Training facilities to external fee-paying customers he has studied relentlessly. As well as acquiring formal training qualifications, Jimmy earned his Human Resources

Management Degree, post-graduate qualifications in Learning and Development, in Personnel and Development and in Management. He also obtained his Master's degree in Strategic Human Resource and became a Chartered Member of the Chartered Institute of Personnel and Development.

In 2010 Jimmy launched Vianet Learning Limited, the UK's leading independent online learning resource dedicated to developing sales practices and selling skills across the UK Motor Industry. Further information can be found at www.vianetlearning.com

With a view to giving back to the community, Jimmy founded the charity the Global Educational Trust (GET) in 2012. GET promotes reading and education worldwide offering free learning and reading resources both at home and abroad. Amongst its many initiatives, in the UK GET provides free books through a nationwide network of "Free Book Shops" and donates resources to educational facilities and community groups. In deprived areas around the world, GET builds educational centres and orphanages offering educational facilities as well as providing bursaries to help students who couldn't otherwise afford it, to further their education. Further details can be found at www.globaleducationaltrust.org

Jimmy is married with three children.

Why I decided to write this book

After a successful sales career, I caught the training bug!

During my years in sales I had read many books written about the subject of selling and sales strategies which had always improved my skills, techniques and ultimately performance.

Having moved to a full-time Learning and Development role, specialising in Sales Training I searched for a book which would do the same for my training abilities, looking for skills and tactics I could employ to further bring the best out of all who attended my courses.

I struggled to find it.

There were many books describing the technical aspects which support learning and development however I wanted something for those of us at the coalface. How could I excel and be the very best learning and development specialist possible. How could I provide Training Excellence and deliver Exceptional Training Programmes?

Undaunted I attended many train the trainer courses and acquired a raft of formal qualifications which would support my increasing skills and experiences. I now want to distil my learning and experience to create the book I would like to purchase.

Whilst this book contains the technical aspects to learning and development you would hope and expect to find I have strived to add the practical aspects to training that you would normally only gain from attendance on training courses or through experience.

As well as covering all aspects of the Identification, Design, Delivery and Evaluation of learning needs, I have tried to offer tips for communicating with groups of people and how to create and fully utilise the right learning environment. Included are strategies for gaining and maintaining participation, the power of yes and how to use repetition without driving your course participants loopy, how to deal with difficult participants, the arc of distortion and aspects of both verbal and non-verbal Communication.

I have included stories, tips, exercises, energisers, ice-breakers and anecdotes that should be invaluable to any trainer seeking to deliver the very best learning experience.

The structure of the book is designed to supply the information allowing a natural progression however, like all good learning experiences it is also modular, being broken into separate sections which can be read and applied in any order.

Enjoy and happy training.

Why training courses fail

Let us begin by characterising failure as it is an incredibly harsh term. The best way to do this is to consider what a great training course would be like.

First of all, from the position of those participating, it should be a learning experience. It should facilitate the acquisition of skills and knowledge. It should be both enjoyable and engaging. It should be stretching and fill those participating with a sense of pride and achievement. It should fulfil the personal objectives of the participants as well as those of the organisation providing the training and encourage the application of the new skills and knowledge after the event. It should reward its participants with an overriding sense of accomplishment. It should be a worthwhile use of their time.

From the trainer's viewpoint the course should be exceptional. The preparation that was committed to the construction of this course should reap great rewards. It should run smoothly, as if it is the hundredth course of its type yet it should feel fresh, as if it is being run for the first time. The trainer should feel touched by the participants, each one being engaged and interested. The trainer should feel energised and have a total belief in the content. There should be eagerness each time a new topic is raised. This should be rewarded with positive body language, smiles and those participating returning early from breaks! The trainer should feel challenged yet knowledgeable, like an expert who is willing to learn. They should feel motivated, confident and in control. The course should receive accolades and positive feedback. Each course should be exceptional. Every course run should be the best course run to date, creating a virtuous spiral of performance.

Whilst the two viewpoints both discuss the ideal training course, they are not mutually exclusive. They are, in fact, interdependent. It would be a challenge for participants to feel engaged and interested if the individual running the course was not engaging or interesting. Likewise, it would be difficult to judge a course as being the best we had ever run if it was not well received.

Whilst anything falling slightly short of this ideal could hardly be considered a failure, it is important to appreciate what should be considered truly successful. This ideal situation, this ideal course should always be the goal. It is what we would want if we were attending as participants. It is what we want to deliver as training professionals.

Unfortunately, as is so often seen, many people fall into the trap of simply "running a training course", training for training's sake or, let's be honest, simply getting through the day without being assaulted!

Even if you haven't run one of these, you've probably experienced one. If you haven't, rest assured some of your course participants have.

This fact creates both a problem and an opportunity. Many of those attending your training course will have experienced poor training in the past.

100% of present behaviour is based on 100% of past experience

Experience refers to the nature of the events someone or something has undergone and it forms our perception of the world.

It is yesterday's experience which governs today's expectation and we tend to behave in line with our expected outcomes.

Basically, people expect their previous experience to be repeated, so, if they have experienced poor training in the past they will expect it again, this time, from you!

This explains why many people attending a training course bring negativity or cynicism which can manifest itself in challenging behaviour.

This creates what many perceive to be a problem, that is, people arriving on the training course with a very negative attitude. I choose to see this, and hope you will too, as a fantastic opportunity.

You get to change their experience and affect their attitude to learning

You only need to be marginally better than average to appear good, if you're good you will appear excellent and if you strive for excellence, the sky is quite literally the limit.

Whilst this is said in jest, it is not a million miles away from the truth. Training, like learning, should be enjoyable. It should be rewarding, and getting a reward is fun. So; in the words of Mother Teresa:

> *"Let no one come before you without leaving better and happier"*

Factors affecting the success of training courses

There are many reasons why a training course may fail:

- o No training/learning need identified
- o The course is not relevant
- o No management support or buy in
- o The course is passing on someone else's bad news
- o The participants have attended bad courses previously, arrive with a negative attitude and this is not confronted by the trainer
- o The course is poorly designed
- o Environment
- o Lack of trainer preparation
- o Poor training skills/style
- o The course is padded due to lack of content (participants always know)
- o Not enough breaks
- o No critical reflection
- o Learning styles not taken into account
- o Confusing delivery
- o Little or no interaction

All of these will contribute to the greatest failure of all:

- o *FAILURE TO ENGAGE THE PARTICIPANTS*

A trip to the cinema

Have you ever been to the cinema where you were really looking forward to seeing the film? You have identified a need and researched a solution. You have waited in eager anticipation and the weekend is upon you. You visit your local multiplex where your every comfort is catered for. You have even parted with your own hard earned cash for the privilege and paid over the odds at the concessions stand. You find a good seat. Your view is un-obstructed. With unabated excitement you settle down to watch the movie.

You have high expectations. Why shouldn't you? The most precious commodity we possess is time and you are dedicating some of yours to watching this movie. The film, in your opinion, turns out to be poor. It just doesn't grab you. Consider the disappointment you feel. How do you refer to the experience when discussing it with others?

Conversely, consider a time where you weren't particularly in the mood for the cinema and for whatever reason, went anyway. Everything is done with a certain amount of apathy, a level of bored acceptance. You probably complain about the prices, the queues and possibly your seat. Someone sits two rows in front of you to your annoyance. The film begins and…..you're hooked! It has grabbed you. From the opening credits to the final scene you're captivated. How will you relay this experience to others?

What has changed?

Well, external factors have an impact. All the issues surrounding the event will affect how you respond to the event itself so it is imperative that they are delivered at the highest level. If the cinema was shabby and the service poor our enjoyment of the film would be affected. Carrying this into a training scenario, from the initial needs analysis through the introductory pack and telephone call to the learning environment and even the chairs, we must commit to delivering an exceptional experience.

Beyond that, the most significant aspect of the day, the main differentiator, the maker of breaker is, of course, you and your course.

Throughout this book we will discuss all aspects of training needs analysis, training design, delivery and evaluation. The primary focus will be on making this the most effective and memorable course our participants have ever attended.

LEARNING

The Psychology of Learning

Helping People Learn Through Training

How Adults Learn

Learning Styles

Sensory Effects on Learning

The Learning Ladder

Introduction

Running effective training programs moves beyond simply imparting information.

Effective training facilitates the acquisition of skills and knowledge. It encourages improvement and development. While it is not a panacea, a "cure all", if used correctly it can better equip a workforce to face their respective challenges, driving goals and targets and should ultimately enhance individual as well as organisational performance. Unfortunately, many training courses fail to achieve their primary objective which should be to motivate learners and stimulate learning.

In order to design and deliver truly effective training courses, workshops or sessions, consideration must first be given to how people learn.

The following chapter begins by examining the psychology of learning, exploring exactly what learning is and how people can be helped to learn through training.

Having considered the general principles involved in learning, the chapter then explores in more detail the specific characteristics of adult learning and the application of these learning theories within the context of designing and delivering effective training programs. Included within this are the effects of individual learning styles, learning preferences and sensory effects on learning.

Enjoy.

The Psychology of Learning

Achieving a better understanding of the process of learning will better equip the training professional for the construction and delivery of effective learning and development activities.

What is learning?

Let's first consider the dictionary definition of learning:

> **learning** *n.* **1.** gain knowledge of or skill in by study; experience, instruction or scholarship. **2.** the act of gaining knowledge, be informed, ascertain, find out

Whilst this appears to be purely a definition of learning within an educational context which most people associate with formal education, it also explains that learning continues long after traditional schooling. Learning continues through work-related training, personal activities and interests. We are even learning when we carry out research prior to making any major purchase.

Psychologists have further broadened the scope of "learning".

Fontana (1988) summarises their work into the following definition:

> ***"Learning is a relatively persistent change in an individual's potential behaviour due to experience."***

Fontana goes on to state that:

"This definition draws attention to three things: first, that learning must change the individual in some way; second, that this change comes about as a result of experience; and third, that this is a change in his or her potential behaviour."

Source:
(Fontana, (1988), *Psychology for Teachers*, British psychological Society/Macmillan, Basingstoke, p. 125)

Learning is achieved when it facilitates a change in an individual's potential behaviour. The change comes about as a result of an experience of some form. Interestingly the definition reinforces that the change is in an individual's *potential* behaviour. Someone may acquire skills or knowledge on a training course and not actually use that learning for several weeks or months, if at all.

So, learning refers to the acquisition of skill and/or knowledge. Yet there are *three* things which will govern whether or not an activity can or will take place:

> ## *Skills, Knowledge* and *Attitude.*

If one of these is absent, then the activity will not take place.

An individual may acquire skills, or indeed already possess them, however if they do not know how to employ them they will not be used. Conversely, an individual can understand the theoretical application of a set of skills yet not have the ability to practically apply them.

Finally, an individual can have both the skills and knowledge, that is, understand how to apply a set of skills and have the ability to utilise them however their attitude may stop them from actually employing them.

So what does this mean?

It means that if our training leads to learning (and let's hope it does!!) we are encouraging people to *change*. Change skills. Change knowledge. The scary step for many people is to acknowledge the fact that for our training to be truly effective it will also facilitate a change of *attitude*.

Most people have experience of training which simply "ticks the box". They have been told that there is a need to acquire new skills and knowledge. They have attended a course, they have acquired the new skills and knowledge and then nothing changes. Consider the motivational impact of putting your heart and soul into acquiring new skills and knowledge only to return and simply continue doing what you have always done.

This is why training often evokes negative responses within some people. People often approach their first training experience with enthusiasm and justifiably high expectations. They expect the training to have an impact on everyday life. If they then experience training and it proves to have little or no impact on their day-to-day life it has a hugely negative impact on their attitude towards future training.

Training should do more than "tick the box". Whilst it is important to do this as an absolute minimum, training should form an integral part of the overall change process and encourage its participants to *apply* the new skills and knowledge to the betterment of themselves and those around them.

People do not fear change; they fear being *changed*

People do not fear change; they fear being *changed*. Improvement, if self-induced, is rarely recognised as change. It is simply a natural progression. So natural it usually goes un-noticed. It is common sense. Unfortunately, common sense is rarely common practise. So, rather than seeing training as an instructional process, simply think about motivating and helping people to learn.

Part of facilitating an effective learning environment is focusing on the motivation of those learners present rather than simply on imparting skills and knowledge.

Good training will facilitate change in an individual's *potential* behaviour. The challenge is to move beyond training and create a learning environment which will facilitate change in an individual's *actual* behaviour.

Helping people learn through Training

Most people who are asked when they last undertook any learning will probably list their schooling, college or perhaps some formal work-based training yet these same people will regularly tune into documentaries on television. The number of documentary channels available is indicative of their popularity however people don't recognise this as learning.

Why? It is because it is engaging.

Topics which would otherwise be inaccessible are beamed into our consciousness with a personal relevance which maintains our interest. Above all it is entertaining. It makes learning fun. In fact, it makes learning so interesting and so much fun it is no-longer perceived as learning.

> ## P = R, Not the Truth!

Where "P" = perception and "R" = reality

So for those people participating in our courses,

Perception = Reality, not necessarily the truth.

Consider the perceptions people have adopted;

Training is traditionally something which is done to you. It is fixed, one-way traffic. Learning on the other hand allows people more control over their own development. This tiny change in language can generate significant change in people's attitude.

Let's consider some dictionary definitions:

> **training** *n.* **1. a.** the process of bringing a person, etc., to an agreed standard of proficiency, etc., by practice and instruction. **learning** *n.* **1.** knowledge gained by study; instruction or scholarship. **2.** the act of gaining knowledge.

Practice and instruction? Or gaining knowledge? Which feels better?

Whilst it may only be semantics, words on a page, the impact upon your sessions, your participants and ultimately you can be substantial. Your approach can mean the difference between engagement or apathy, commitment or compliance.

The best way to view training, if you want to be really good and most of all, well respected:

> **Training is a means of helping people learn**

So, let's consider how adults learn.

How adults learn

If training is to be applied as a means of helping people learn, it is first important to understand the manner in which learning takes place, the distinct processes involved in the acquisition of skill, knowledge or a change in attitude.

Alan Rogers (2003), drawing on the work of those studying the learning of languages set out two contrasting approaches to learning:

- **Task-conscious**
- **Learning-conscious**

Task-conscious or acquisition learning

Task-conscious or acquisition learning is learning which is seen as going on all the time, for example the learning involved in bringing up children or in running a home. It is often referred to as unconscious or implicit learning.

Learning-conscious or formalised learning

Formalised learning arises from the process of facilitated learning. To this extent there is a consciousness of learning. People are aware that the task in which they are engaged entails learning. Learning itself is the task and involves guided episodes of learning.

It is clear that these contrasting ways of learning are not mutually exclusive and so can occur at the same time. Both are present in traditional education and in families. Whilst acquisition learning should occur as a by-product of our organised sessions we will explore the more formal aspects of learning with a view to creating some structure and/or best practises which can be applied in a general context to facilitate learning within our formal sessions.

Following are four key theories on learning:

- behaviourist learning theory

- cognitive learning theory

- humanistic learning theory

- social/situational learning theory

Behaviourist learning theory

John B. Watson is generally credited as the first behaviourist. He stated that the inner experiences which form the focus of psychology were not observable and therefore could not be properly studied.

Watson turned to laboratory experimentation which resulted in the generation of the *stimulus-response model*. Aspects of the environment are seen as providing stimuli to which individuals develop responses.

Researchers like Edward L. Thorndike built upon these foundations developing a Stimulus-Response theory of learning. He noted that responses, or behaviours, were strengthened or weakened by the consequences of behaviour.

The importance of reinforcement

This notion was refined by B.H. Skinner and is perhaps better known as ***operant conditioning***. The focus of Operant conditioning is reinforcement. Much like the pleasure/pain principle, he theorised that people will be drawn to pleasurable activities and try to avoid painful ones. In essence, behaviour can be influenced by reinforcing what you want people to do again and ignoring or punishing what you want people to stop doing.

In terms of learning, according to James Hartley there are four key principles:

- *Activity*

- *Repetition, Generalisation and Discrimination*

- *Reinforcement*

- *Learning is helped when objectives are clear*

Activity

Learning is better when the learner is active rather than passive. Many theories, some discussed further in this book, rely on the importance of activity.

Repetition, generalisation and discrimination

Frequent practice and practice in varied contexts is necessary for learning to take place. As we hear time and time again, practise or repletion is required for skill development. In fact, skills will not be acquired without frequent practice.

Reinforcement

Positive reinforcement in the form of rewards and successes are preferable to negative events like punishments and failures.

Learning is helped when objectives are clear

Learning is facilitated when it is undertaken with a clear intent. Learning requires clear goals and measurable outcomes.

Those who look to behaviourism in training will generally frame their activities by behavioural objectives e.g. 'By the end of this session participants will be able to...'.

Cognitive learning theory

Many psychologists, especially Gestalt psychologists, believed that perceptions or images should be approached as a pattern or as a whole rather than as a sum of the component parts. In fact, "Gestalt" is actually the German word for order, meaning configuration or pattern.

This new school of thought had a profound effect on the way that many psychologists viewed learning. Where behaviourists looked to the environment, those drawing on Gestalt turned to the individual's mental processes, with "cognition" - the act or process of knowing.

Whilst recognising the contribution of environment, researchers explored changes in internal cognitive structure and how mental processes could be linked to learning.

James Hartley (1998) highlighted some of the key principles of learning associated with cognitive psychology. He believed that:

- Instruction should be well-organised and clearly structured

- The perceptual features of the task are important

- Prior knowledge is important

- Differences between individuals are important as they have a significant impact on learning

- Cognitive feedback about success/failure is important

Instruction should be well-organised and clearly structured

As learning is seen as a cognitive process, well-organised materials are easier to learn and to remember. Subject matters are said to have logical relationships between key ideas and concepts which link the parts together.

The perceptual features of the task are important

The way an issue or task is displayed is important if learners are to understand it.

Prior knowledge is important

People learn by association. Things must fit with what is already known if it is to be learnt.

Differences between individuals are important as they will affect learning

Learning is influenced by differences in cognitive style or methods of approach.

Cognitive feedback about success/failure is important

Positive feedback has a significant impact on learning. Reinforcement can be as simple as praise or the giving of information rather than offering a reward.

Humanistic learning theory

This approach to learning focusses on the human potential for growth and the desire for improvement. Humanistic learning theory accounts for personal freedom, choice, motivations and feelings.

Perhaps the best known example is Abraham Maslow's work in the area of motivation theory, in which he constructed his hierarchy of needs. Maslow ranked five distinct needs ranging from physiological needs at the lowest level through to self-actualisation. We are motivated to satisfy our needs. Only when the lower needs are met is it possible to fully move on to the next level. A motivational need at the lower level is always stronger than those at higher levels.

Maslow's hierarchy of needs:

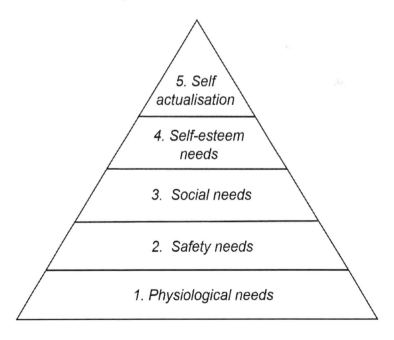

Physiological needs

Physiological refers to our very basic needs such as thirst, hunger, sleep, relaxation and bodily integrity. These needs must first be satisfied before we can progress to the next level.

From a training perspective, the challenge of getting the best from our participants diminishes in line with their thirst, hunger or tiredness!

Safety needs

This level of need requires a predictable and orderly world. If these are not satisfied people will look to organise their worlds to provide for the greatest degree of safety and security. Safety does not necessarily refer simply to physical safety. Individuals tend to find learning more difficult when feeling threatened or bullied. In order to learn, individuals required emotional as well as physical safety.

Social needs

People like to fit in. They will seek warm, loving and friendly relationships. They have an innate need or desire to feel part of a group or team.

Self-esteem needs

As well as fitting in, individuals also like to stand out perhaps explaining why praise and recognition play such a significant part in the learning process. Here the individual has the desire for strength, achievement, mastery and competence. This level of need will also involve confidence, independence, reputation and prestige.

Self-actualisation

Here the individual will endeavour to demonstrate full use and expression of talents, capacities and potential. From a learning perspective, this can be achieved by using their skills to help others and excel.

If you consider the lead singer of a struggling band as they achieve stardom:

With money and fame they begin at the base level, indulging in food, drink and stimulants. As the money rolls in they satisfy their need for safety and body guards or an entourage are in tow. Being recognised as part of the band helps with their social needs however they probably also blog on line or have a fan club. As lead singer not only are they a member of the band, they are the focal member, standing out and achieving self-esteem needs with attention from adoring fans. Having satisfied their base needs and the need to feel safe as well as their social needs and self-esteem needs they can "give back" and start a charity or foundation, using their talents for the betterment of humanity.

The application of a hierarchy of needs within training

Maslow's model highlights those needs particular to the participants of our training programs. Chapter 5 "Delivering Training Programs" considers the effects and practicalities of creating the right environment, with a view to first satisfying the individuals physiological and safety needs. The chapter also considers the requirement to satisfy social needs when working with a group and explores the role of training in achievement, mastery and competence helping to satisfy self-esteem needs.

Those attaining self-actualisation are able to submit to social regulation without losing their own integrity or personal independence. They can follow a social norm without failure to see or consider other possibilities.

As such, learning can be seen as a form of self-actualisation as it contributes to overall psychological health.

Experiential Learning

Carl Rogers, considered the father of experiential learning, saw the following elements as being involved in experiential learning:

- **Personal involvement**

Both feeling and cognitive aspects are incorporated into the learning event.

- **It is self-initiated**

The motivation for learning comes from within. The learner is not passive.

- **It is pervasive**

It makes a difference in the behaviour, the attitudes, perhaps even the personality of the learner.

- **It is evaluated by the learner**

The learner assesses to what extent the activity is meeting their needs.

- **Its essence is meaning**

When such learning takes place, the element of meaning to the learner is built into the whole experience. (Rogers, 1983)

The Experiential Learning Cycle

Kolb (1984), inspired by the work of Kurt Lewin, provided one of the most useful descriptive models of the adult learning process.

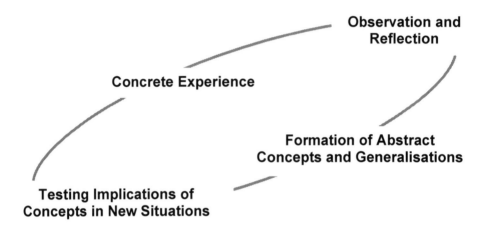

This cyclical approach suggests that experiential learning is a looped process containing four distinct stages:

Concrete Experience is followed by personal **reflection** on that experience. In other words, having "done something", we benefit from thinking about what we have done. Reviewing our performance and success or failure.

Following this the learner will enter a period of **abstract conceptualisation** where they will derive a set of general rules describing the experience or they will apply known theories to it. So having done something and thought about what it is that they have done, they now consider "what could I do differently? How could my performance be improved?"

This will lead to active **experimentation** where methods for modifying the next occurrence of this experience will be constructed. Having established new theories, they will actively try some of them out which will lead, in turn, to the next Concrete Experience.

All this may happen in a relatively short period of time or over days, weeks or even months, depending on the topic. There may also be a "wheels within wheels" process happening at the same time.

In order for learning to be effective, focus is required in each area of the experiential learning cycle.

This model can be used to ensure that learning activities are designed to give full value to each stage of the process.

Social/Situational Learning Theory

Social learning theory puts forward the view that people learn from observing other people. It determines that we can learn from other people's mistakes! As well as their successes of course. It was behaviourists who first considered how people learned through observation. Observation allows people to see the consequences of other people's behaviours. An idea of what might result by acting in a similar way may be formed.

Most human behaviour is learned through observation and modelling.

Observing behaviour, remembering it in the form of a model or paradigm and then rehearsing its application in different situations are key aspects of observational learning.

Summary

Different people learn in different ways in different circumstances. There is benefit in employing the positive aspects of each of these learning theories.

The following combines the core principles of learning theory and underpins effective course design:

Objectives:

Each session should begin with clear and specific objectives

Motivation:

The learner should be engaged and motivated to learn

Structure:

All instruction should be clearly structured and well organised

Understandable:

All topics and issues should be presented in a way which is easy to understand

Activity:

Activity should be encouraged in all learning events

Experiential Learning:

Learners should be encouraged through all aspects of the Experiential Learning Cycle

Feedback:

Feedback should be given regarding successes and areas of development

Repetition:

Repetition is the mother of all learning. Learners should have the opportunity for frequent practise and practise in varied contexts

Reinforcement:

Learners will receive positive reinforcement in the form of rewards and successes

Learner Evaluation:

The learner is encouraged to evaluate to what extent the activity is meeting their needs

Observation:

Learners will be given the opportunity to observe and model behaviours

Learning differences:

Sessions will include a variety of learning approaches and activities

This final point highlights the fact that different people prefer to learn in different ways.

Let's have a look at different learning preferences, or styles.

Learning styles

Great minds don't all think alike!

Many people attend university each year. Each student has the same access to materials, the same access to lectures and the same access to information yet not all will pass and those that do attain different grades.

Likewise, many people attend night classes to study a variety of topics from languages to the acquisition or improvement of IT skills. Like those attending university, all have access to the same information yet each will produce radically different results.

One reason for this discrepancy in success is the varying levels of hard work and dedication, of commitment demonstrated by each individual. Another issue affecting learning success is the way in which individuals prefer to learn.

Whilst each of the preceding theories of learning describes general approaches to learning, a major factor which impacts on an individual's ability to learn is the manner in which they prefer to acquire skills or knowledge, known as their learning style or preference.

All great minds don't think alike!

Different people prefer to learn in different ways. What stimulates one individual will bore another, what fascinates one, frustrates the other.

An understanding of learning styles or learning preferences can help explain why some learning seems difficult, almost like a chore while other learning is so enjoyable it appears effortless. The important distinction is that enjoyable, stimulating learning *still requires effort*; it just doesn't feel like it.

People find it very easy to do what they want to do and we want to do the things we enjoy. An obvious statement as it is a statement of fact.

> ## We find it easy to do the things we enjoy!

This statement still holds true when we consider learning.

If we remove the term learning and just consider it as an activity, if we enjoy the activity, if it stimulates and excites us, we are more inclined to do it, do it well and, more importantly, keep doing it. If we don't enjoy the activity, if it fails to stimulate we become bored and frustrated. We procrastinate and become very resistant and negative. So our learning preference actually affects our ability to demonstrate the hard work and commitment required to be successful. If the learning stimulates we are encouraged to work hard and do so freely. If we are not stimulated by the learning activity, learning actually becomes difficult and is considered hard work.

If as trainers we can tap into that which stimulates individuals and groups and make learning fun and interesting, we can also make learning easy! Training which accounts for the manner in which people like to learn stimulates and motivates learners. It makes learning enjoyable and rewarding for the learners and trainer alike.

The rewards received are often exponentially greater than the effort required because it simply doesn't feel like effort when we are doing what we want.

So, what are learning styles?

The learning styles

Some people prefer to learn through activity, others from reflection. Some prefer to theorise and others would rather put these theories into practice. An individual's preferred style of learning will affect the learning environment in which they will flourish.

Peter Honey and Alan Mumford developed their learning styles system as a variation on the Kolb model while working on a project for the Chloride Corporation in the 1970's. In their Learning Styles Questionnaire Honey and Mumford describe four distinct learning styles:

1. *The Activist*

2. *The Reflector*

3. *The Theorist*

4. *The Pragmatist*

The Activist

Unsurprisingly Activists enjoy activity, that is, they love doing and they adore doing new things. As such, they involve themselves fully and without bias in new experiences and enjoy the here and now.

Activists particularly enjoy doing anything new. As a result they tend to be open-minded rather than sceptical which makes them enthusiastic about anything new. They are happy to be dominated by immediate experiences immersing themselves fully in new activities.

Activists are often recognised as "throwing caution to the wind". They leap in where angels fear to tread with the words "I'll try anything once".

They enjoy the "doing" and their days are filled with activity. As soon as the excitement from one activity has dissipated, they are busy looking for the next "shiny new thing".

Whilst they tend to thrive on the challenge of new experiences, they are bored with their subsequent implementation and any longer term consolidation.

Activists revel in short term crisis and firefighting, tackling problems by brainstorming. They are gregarious people constantly involving themselves with others although in doing so, they will tend to hog the limelight.

As such they are the life and soul of the party, seeking to centre all activities on themselves.

Learning considerations:

Positive Attributes:

The Activist is both flexible and open minded.
They are happy to be exposed to new situations.
Activists will have a go and are always ready to join in.
The Activist is optimistic about anything new and as such is unlikely to resist change.

Areas to be aware of:

Activists are prone to taking unnecessary risks.
The Activist has a tendency to take the immediately obvious action invariably without thinking.
Activists will rush headlong into an action or activity with little thought or preparation.
The Activist is intent on doing rather than thinking about what to do and as such may repeat the same mistake.
The Activists will want to hog the limelight.
The desire for action will generally result in the Activist doing too much of the activity themselves.
The Activist will ultimately get bored with implementation and consequently very little will come to fruition.

Key questions considered by the activist prior to learning:

- Will I learn something new?
- Will there be a variety of different activities?
- Will I be allowed to let my hair down and have fun?
- Will I be allowed to make mistakes?
- Will there be other like-minded people to mix with?

The Reflector

Like a mirror or shiny surface the Reflector prefers to "reflect" back on information provided.

Reflectors prefer to take a step back from the activity to ponder experiences and observe from many different perspectives.

They collect data both first hand and from others, and will mull it over thoroughly, carefully considering all the information at hand before coming to any conclusion. The thorough collection and analysis of data about experiences and events is what counts so the Reflector tends to postpone reaching definitive conclusions for as long as possible.

Their philosophy is to be cautious, leaving no stone unturned. The motto of the Reflector would be: "Look before you leap" and "sleep on it". Reflectors are thoughtful people who like to consider all possible angles and implications before making any decision or move.

The preference of the Reflector is to take a back seat in meetings and discussions, enjoying observing other people in action. They listen to others and get the drift of the discussion before making their own points.

Reflectors tend to adopt a low profile and have a slightly distant, tolerant, unruffled air about them. When they act it is as part of a wide picture which includes the past as well as the present the observations of others along with their own.

Learning considerations:

Positive attributes:

Reflectors are very careful thoroughly analysing information prior to making any decision.

Reflectors are methodical in their analysis of all situations.

Reflectors are very thoughtful. They are good at listening to others and assimilating information.

Reflectors will rarely jump to conclusions.

Areas to be aware of:

Reflectors are rather staid and have a tendency to hold back from direct participation.

Reflectors are often slow to make decisions and will deliberate for a long time when making up their minds.

Reflectors have a tendency to be too cautious and as such will not take many risks.

Reflectors rarely display assertion. They are not particularly forthcoming and rarely engage in "small talk".

Key questions considered by the reflector prior to learning

- Will I be given adequate time to think things through?
- Will there be the opportunity and resource available to assemble all the relevant information?
- Will there be a wide cross-section of people with a variety of views?
- Will I be under pressure to get things done quickly?
- Will I be forced to "join in"?

The Theorist

Theorists adapt and integrate observations into complex, logically sound theories. They think problems through in a vertical, step by step logical way.

The Theorist will assimilate disparate facts into coherent theories. They tend to be perfectionists who won't rest easy until things are tidy and fit into their rational scheme. They like to analyse and synthesise. They are keen on basic assumptions, principles, theories, models and systems thinking.

The Theorists philosophy prizes rationality and logic thinking "If it's logical it's good". Questions they frequently ask are:
"Does it make sense?"
"How does this fit with that?"
"What are the basic assumptions?"

Theorists tend to be detached, analytic and dedicated to rational objectivity rather than anything subjective or ambiguous. Their approach to problems is consistently logical. This is their "mental set" and they rigidly reject anything that doesn't fit with it.

Theorists prefer to maximise certainty and feel uncomfortable with subjective judgements, lateral thinking and anything flippant.

Learning considerations:

Positive attributes:

The Theorist is a logical "vertical" thinker who adopts a linear approach.
Theorists are always rational and remain objective.
Theorists are good at asking probing questions.
Theorists adopt a disciplined approach.

Areas to be aware of:

Theorists are restricted in their ability to apply lateral thinking.
Their desire for order gives them a low tolerance for uncertainty and ambiguity.
Theorists are intolerant of anything subjective or intuitive.

Key questions considered by the theorist prior to learning

- Will there be opportunities to ask questions?
- Is there a clear structure and purpose?
- Will I encounter complex ideas and concepts that will stretch me?
- Are the approaches to be used and concepts to be explored "valid"?
- Will there be other people of similar calibre to myself?

The Pragmatist

The Pragmatist is keen to try out new ideas, techniques or theories to see if they work in practice. They will actively search for ideas and concepts and take every opportunity to experiment and apply the principles.

Much like the Activist, the Pragmatists are "doers" and like to get on with things acting quickly and confidently on any ideas that attract them. They are very direct and become impatient with ruminating, open-ended discussions. They are practical, down to earth people who enjoy making practical decisions and problem solving.

Pragmatists see problems as opportunities or challenges. They will always search for a better way of doing things and will very often find it.

Learning considerations:

Positive attributes:

Pragmatists are very practical, down to earth and realistic.
Actively seek out opportunities to test things in real life situations.
They are straight talking and direct.
Pragmatists are business like, getting straight to the point.

Areas to be aware of:

Pragmatists have a tendency to reject anything which does not have obvious applications.
They are not very interested in theory or basic principles.
Pragmatists have a tendency to seize on the first expedient solution.
They are impatient and become frustrated with long discussion.

They can be task rather than people oriented.

Key questions to ask the Pragmatist prior to learning

- Will there be opportunity to practice and experiment?
- Will there be lot of practical tips and techniques?
- Will we be addressing real problems?
- Will I be mixing with "hands-on" experts who have shown they can do it themselves?

Summary

This focus on learning theories and learning styles has major implications for the learning and development process. This is particularly important when choosing learning techniques and technology to be employed.

For example, activists are keen to put ideas into practice at the earliest possible opportunity and will get frustrated if too much time is spent reviewing previous learning situations where as the reflector requires time after the situation to consider all the information available in order to evaluate its impact.

Our learning style gives an indication of the learning activities with which we would prefer to engage. Unless encouraged otherwise, the reflector will resist the action and activity chosen by the Activist. The Pragmatist will grow frustrated with the preferred discourse and debate of the theorist whose lack of direct action will create barriers for the Activists and so, on it goes.

The automatic assumption may be to create learning strategies that allow each learning style to play to its own particular strength however this will happen automatically and often leads to neglected learning opportunities. Learning strategies should be created which encourage each individual to work around the experiential learning cycle, incorporating learning opportunities which would otherwise be resisted.

In generic terms these learning styles prove an important consideration when designing learning and development opportunities. Rarely do people fall totally into one category and even if they did, having a group of people who all fall totally into one of these categories would be unlikely. As such, a mix of learning strategies are required if we are to encourage each individual to apply their inherent skills and engage everyone in a more efficient learning experience.

Sensory effects on Learning

Not surprisingly people learn by processing the information they receive and they receive information using their primary senses. Whilst the gustatory and olfactory (taste and smell) senses are employed when learning, they are rarely described separately.

How we process information which is acquired using the remaining three primary senses of visual, auditory and kinaesthetic will affect our learning preferences.

Whilst we all employ all of the senses we have available to us, when it comes to the manner in which we process information and how it affects our approach to learning, learners, irrespective of learning style, can also be split into three primary categories:

- **Visual learners**

- **Auditory learners**

- **Kinaesthetic learners**

Visual Learners

Learn through seeing...

These learners need to see your body language and facial expression to fully understand the session content and what, exactly, you may be trying to help them develop.

They may try to avoid visual obstructions and so tend to sit at the front of the room, or directly in front of you. They tend to be highly visual people and think in pictures. As such they will learn best from visual displays such as PowerPoint, videos, flipcharts and hand-outs.

During the session these learners will often take detailed notes which helps them absorb the information although interestingly, some will rarely refer back to them and may never read them again.

Visual learners can be divided into two distinct categories:

- **Visual/verbal learners**
- **Visual/non-verbal learners**

Visual/verbal learners

This learner learns best when information is presented visually in a written language format. They benefit when the flip chart, whiteboard or projected screen are used to list the essential points of a session.

The visual/verbal learner prefers to have a general idea of the flow of the session or day and as such, will benefit from the use of an agenda or session "route map".

These learners will benefit from information obtained from books and comprehensive session notes. They tend to like to study on their own and in a quiet room.

They often see information "in their mind's eye" when they are trying to remember something.

Visual/Nonverbal Learners

The visual/nonverbal learner learns best when information is presented visually and pictorially. During sessions they benefit when information is presented in using films, videos, diagrams and illustrations.

They will draw information from the pictures and diagrams in textbooks.

When trying to remember something, they can often visualise a picture of it in their mind. They may have an artistic side that enjoys activities having to do with visual art and design.

Auditory Learners

Learn through listening...

Auditory learners learn best during verbal sessions, discussions, by talking things through and listening to what others have to say. They interpret the underlying meanings of speech through listening to tone of voice, pitch, speed and other nuances.

Written information may have little meaning until it is heard. These learners often benefit from reading text aloud and listening to, rather than reading, transcripts. As such, the auditory learner benefits from information being presented in an oral language format.

During sessions, they benefit from listening to information being presented, participating in group discussions and from obtaining information via audio equipment such as CDs.

When trying to remember something, they can often "hear" the way they originally heard the information, or the way they previously repeated it out loud.

They learn best when interacting with others in an exchange of listening and speaking.

Kinaesthetic Learners

Learn through moving, touching and doing...

Kinaesthetic people learn best when using a hands-on approach, actively exploring the physical world around them. They may find it difficult or frustrating to sit still for long periods and may become distracted by their need for activity. They learn best when they can be physically active in the learning environment and benefit from the use of demonstrations, "hands on" learning experiences and activity.

Learning style considerations

There is no right or wrong, good or bad learning style. It is purely a preference. It has nothing to do with intelligence. It has everything to do with how an individual's brain processes information which has been learned in order to store that information. As everyone learns differently, taking into account these different learning preferences will help make our learning experiences more effective and enjoyable.

Ensuring a mix of learning experiences and strategies will help keep the learning fresh and appeal to a cross-section of participants. Whilst the following categorises strategies which will appeal to distinct learning preferences, employing any or all of the strategies will cater for the diverse participants you can expect on any given course.

Visual Learners:

Visual Stimulation:

- Visual stimulation is important so to make learning easier, make written information bright and interesting to look at.
- Make use of "colour coding" when presenting new information in any handouts or session notes.

Facilitate note taking:

- Provide highlighter pens and writing pens of different colours and gradients and encourage the participants to make use of them when making their notes.

- Encourage participants to highlight different information in contrasting colours.
- Encourage the learners to write out sentences and phrases that summarise key information discussed within the session.

Flashcards:

- Encourage the participants to create flashcards using different colours and highlighter pens to emphasise key items.
- Encourage the learners to draw symbols and pictures on the cards.
- Try to limit the amount of information per card so their mind can take a mental "picture" or "snap-shot" of the information.

Diagrammatical Presentation of Information:

- When the learning information is presented using diagrams or illustrations, write out explanations of the information or issue handouts.

Break into manageable chunks:

- When a problem involves a sequence of steps, write out in detail how to do each step. Distribute handouts which are bright, interesting and easy to read. Make charts to organise the information.
- Encourage the learners to take note during the session.

Vary the Presentation Media:

- Make use of a whiteboard and flip chart. Encourage the use of mnemonics, acronyms and mind maps.

Memory Techniques:

- Ask the participants to organise the material.
- Use visual analogies. Employee highly descriptive storytelling.
- When the learning involves a sequence of steps, create flow charts.
- As much as possible, translate words and ideas into symbols, pictures, and diagrams.

Auditory Learners:

Use Group work:

- Encourage learners to study in groups.
- Break out into groups and complete exercise/syndicate work.

Verbal Participation:

- Encourage the learners to explain the material to you as if you were the participant.
- Ask them to read explanations out loud.
- Encourage the participants to talk out loud when learning information. Whilst unusual at first this technique greatly enhances recall.
- Encourage the learners to "talk their way" through the new information.

- Ask the learners to state the problem in their own words.

Memory techniques:

- Ask the learners to make up a song or poem incorporating the subject matter. This against sounds a little strange however how many of us can remember the colours of the rainbow if we begin "red and yellow and… " or that "I before e except after c and except when the sound is a" so, the "crazier" the better.
- Encourage the learner to make up acronyms and used mnemonics. "Richard of York gave battle in vain" is a way in which many of us remember the spectrum colours (from the first letter of each word - red, orange, yellow, green, blue, indigo and violet)
- To learn a sequence of steps, get them to write them out in sentence form and read them out loud.

Kinaesthetic Learners:

Positioning:

- Encourage the learner to sit near the front of the room and take notes during the sessions.
- Ask them to stand while they explain something.
- Create a situation that involves them moving in their chairs or from their chairs altogether. Even a raised hand will create sufficient change to their physiology. Ask a question "who has…" or "who agrees that…." and raise your hand. Those who agree will do likewise.

Key words:

- Encourage them to jot down key words and draw pictures or make charts to help them remember the information they are receiving.
- Encourage them to write while they are reading or talking.

Employ touch:

- Employ learning methods which make their learning tangible. Use something they can put their hands on, make a model that illustrates a key concept.
- Leave stress balls/toys on the desk.
- Make use of a computer to reinforce learning through the sense of touch.
- Encourage them to pick up the book/handout as they are reading or talking.

Flashcards:

- To learn a sequence of steps, encourage the participants to make flashcards for each step. Arrange the cards on a table top to represent the correct sequence. Put words, symbols, or pictures on the flashcards -- anything that helps them remember the information. Use highlighter pens in contrasting colours to emphasize important points. Limit the amount of information per card to aid recall. Practice putting the cards in order until the sequence becomes automatic.

Encourage verbal and vocal techniques:

- Encourage the learner to exaggerate lip movements in front of a mirror.
- Encourage them to use syncopation and rhythm when speaking or explaining something.
- Use gestures when giving explanations and encourage the learners to do the same.

The Learning Ladder

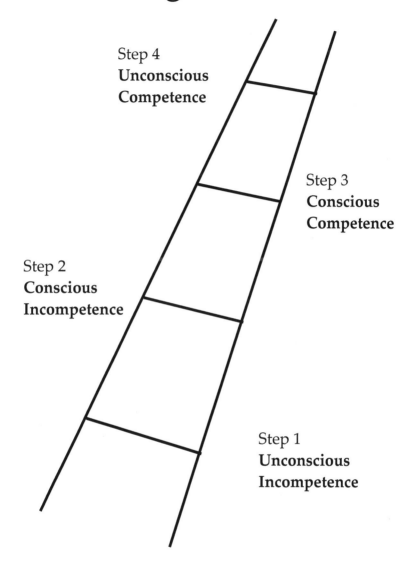

Step 4
**Unconscious
Competence**

Step 3
**Conscious
Competence**

Step 2
**Conscious
Incompetence**

Step 1
**Unconscious
Incompetence**

The Learning Ladder details the process and stages of learning a new skill whether it is behavioural, a new ability or a new technique. It is a simple explanation of how we learn, and a useful reminder of the need to train people in stages.

Unconscious Incompetence

The learner or trainee begins on step 1 in a state of "unconscious incompetence". They are not even aware of the existence or relevance of the skill area and as such are unaware of the fact that they have a particular deficiency in this area.

The learner must become conscious of their incompetence before development of the new skill or learning can begin. As such, the primary aim of the learning is to move the individual onto the "conscious competence" step. This is accomplished by raising awareness often by demonstrating the skill or ability and the benefit that it will bring to the individuals effectiveness.

Conscious Incompetence

The learner has become aware of the relevance and existence of the skill or ability. As such, the learner is now also aware of their deficiency in this area. The learner should now realise that by improving their skill ability in this area they will improve their effectiveness. Ideally knowledge of the skills gap is created when the learner has a measure of the extent of their deficiency in the relevant skill area and a measure of what level of skill is required in order for them to achieve their own competence level. Ideally the learner will make a commitment to learn and then practised a new skill or ability and to move to the "conscious competence" step.

Conscious Competence

The learner achieves "conscious competence" in the skill area when they can perform reliably and that will. Whilst they can perform the task the learner will still need to concentrate in order to perform. As such the task is completed on a conscious level and so the learner will not reliably be able to perform the skill unless they are consciously thinking about it, the skill is not yet automatic, it has not become "second nature". Practise of the new skill is now required in order to become "unconsciously competent". Practise is the single most effective method of transcending from step three to step four.

Unconscious Competence

The skill has become so practised that it has now entered the unconscious parts of the brain. It has become 'second nature' and can be performed without conscious thought or determined focus. It becomes possible for skills to be completed while performing other the tasks.

Training issues

Trainers commonly assume that learners are already on step 2, conscious incompetence, and focus their efforts towards achieving step three when often learners are actually still on step one.

The trainer assumes the learner is aware of the existence of this skill deficiency and the subsequent benefit to be derived from its acquisition. If a learner is on step one "unconscious incompetence" they will not be able to address achieving conscious competence until they have become consciously and fully aware of their own incompetence. This is a fundamental reason for the failure of many training sessions.

It is essential to establish awareness of a development or training need, i.e. establish conscious incompetence prior to attempting to impart the knowledge, or perform training of the skills necessary to move learners from step two to step three (conscious incompetence to conscious competence).
If awareness of a skill and deficiency does not exist the learner will simply not see the need for learning. People only respond to training when they are aware of their own need for it, and the personal benefit they will derive from completing it.

Summary

Learning involves stimulating change in an individual's potential behaviour and in adults, is brought about by experience.

Each of the four key theories on learning, behaviourist, cognitive, humanistic and social/situational learning theories have attributes which can be applied positively within training to stimulate learning.

Behaviourist learning theory encourages repetition and reinforcement.

Cognitive learning theory focuses on the act or process of knowing and encourages a structured, well organised approach to learning which is supported by feedback.

Humanistic learning theory focuses on the human potential for growth emphasising personal freedom and choice and so highlighting the need for individuals to be motivated to learn.

The social/situational learning theory encourages observation and modelling as part of the learning process.

The ability of different individuals to learning different circumstances will also be affected by their learning style or preference as well is the way in which they prefer to process information whether that be visually, auditory or kinaesthetically.

As different people learn in different ways in different circumstances there is benefiting employing the positive aspects of each of these learning theories within the context of course design and delivery.

All of these considerations will be applied in the construction of training programs.

So, what is training?

TRAINING

What is training?

The distinction between Training, Coaching and
Presenting

The training cycle

Introduction

Having considered exactly what learning is, we can begin establishing how people can actually be helped to learn through the application of training and development activities.

The following chapter determines exactly what is meant by training and how it differs from coaching and presenting. It goes on to divide training into its constituent parts and establishes a process model which is applicable to all learning and development activities.

Subsequent chapters will then examine each of these process sections in turn, exploring each in detail and offering practical steps for their application within any training program.

What is training?

Well, if we this time take the dictionary definition of training we see:

> **training** *n.* **1. a.** the process of bringing a person, etc., to an agreed standard of proficiency, etc., by practice and instruction.

Whilst this is only a very basic description it is evident that the emphasis is on training bringing about a change in an individual's performance.

Effective training facilitates the acquisition of or a change in; *skills, knowledge* and *attitude* imparting a way of thinking as well as a way of doing.

The effects brought about when there is an absence of training and development are often self-evident. Arising symptoms often include haphazard work, repetition of work due to errors, delays and poor performance, low quality standards and a failure to maintain rules and procedures. Often, more subtle signs begin to show including absenteeism, poor communication, a limited sense of responsibility, low morale and a lack of interest and motivation at work.

A well-trained person should be better equipped to deal with their day-to-day duties and activities. They should be able to face problems and issues with confidence, working well as an individual or as part of a team. Well-constructed and appropriate training should lead to better and happier people in all parts of the organisation.

Children are taught | Adults are trained

There is an important distinction between learning in children and in adults.

Pedagogy describes the learning by and instruction of children, "Ped" being derived from the Greek word for Child and "gogy" from the Greek word for learning. Whilst it refers to learning, pedagogy actually means the arts and science of teaching children.

Pedagogy is biased towards education rather than training as it is associated mainly with the development of knowledge on topics when their previous learning exists.

Andragogical refers to adult learning, "Andra" been derived from the Greek word for man. It takes into account the fact that adults have accumulated a wealth of experience and knowledge and stresses the importance of building on the foundation of previous learning gained through life's experiences.

Andragogical recognises the fact that adults do not need to be "taught" in the traditional sense and that they neither need, nor will they readily accept, learning which is imposed upon them. Provided a need has been established and subsequent benefits have been highlighted, adult learners will act as partners in the learning process. Andragogical is learner centred, recognising the participation of learners in setting instructional objectives and defining their own learning needs.

So, what is the difference between training, coaching and presenting?

The distinction between Training, Coaching and Presenting

In brief:

Presentations impart **information**

Training facilitates **learning**

Coaching enhances **performance**

Presentation $\Longrightarrow$ Information

Training $\Longrightarrow$ Learning

Coaching $\Longrightarrow$ Performance

Presentation:
Presentations are made to a group
Little or no interaction
Information passed on
No validation

Training:
Training delivered to a group
Interaction greatly increased
New Learning facilitated

Coaching:
One to one
Wholly interactive
Performance improvement

Presentations pass on information to groups of people. With the exception of questions which are generally off-set to the end of the presentation and restricted to the subject topic, there is no interaction.

The information flow is one way. Whilst presentations should be structured to allow the information to be easily understood, there is no requirement to confirm how the information has been received. As such, understanding or application of the information is rarely validated.

New or existing information can be delivered to an audience with varying skill levels and understanding.

Training on the other hand facilitates the learning of new concepts, ideas, skills or knowledge. Whilst it is still delivered to a group, the numbers are restricted and the format allows for increased interaction.

Training can be centred on either the trainer or those participating. A Trainer centred approach involves information being delivered by the trainer to the group whereas participant centred training is more group based. The trainer takes a more facilitation based role with exercises and group activities allowing for a more guided learning approach.

Coaching is one to one. Its focus is on developing existing skills and knowledge. As such, it helps the participant do something they already do, better. It is wholly interactive with the participant being encouraged to develop their existing performance. As each individual will have one or more learning preference, the temptation is to repeat the areas of learning we enjoy or with which we feel comfortable. Effective coaching will invariably facilitate activity in all areas of the learning cycle. Participants are generally guided through each area of the experiential learning cycle with the use of questioning and encouragement.

The training cycle

The training cycle is a systematic approach to training and development. It represents the steps involved in creating and delivering effective training and development Strategies.

Training and development can be divided into four distinct stages:

- **Identification**

- **Design**

- **Delivery**

- **Evaluation**

Identification

The initial stage of the training cycle is the identification of training needs. Prior to any training programme being designed or delivered, it is first important to determine what is to be trained. What learning needs exist? What issues require a resolution?

This stage identifies the needs of both the business and the participants which are to be met by the training programme.

Design

Identification of the training needs will allow for objectives of the training programme to be constructed.

With a clear set of objectives, it is now possible to design a training programme which will satisfy the training needs identified and better equip the business to meet its objectives.

Delivery

The training programme can now be delivered.

Evaluation

It is now important to measure the effectiveness of the training programme by measuring it against the initial objectives. There are several distinct levels of evaluation which measure such outcomes as participant satisfaction, participant attainment of skills or knowledge, application of these on return to the workplace and impact on business strategy and objectives.

The four stages of identification, design, delivery and evaluation form a cyclical process:

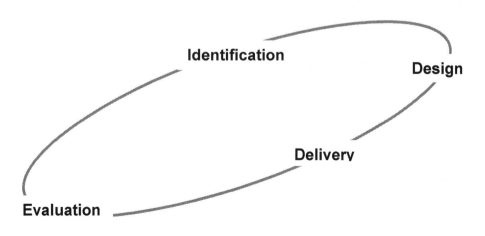

Identification

Design

Delivery

Evaluation

The cycle reflects the fact that training can be viewed as an overall process rather than simply the constituent parts in isolation. The outcome of one stage provides the inputs to the next and the absence of any stage will undermine the overall effectiveness of the process.

The training cycle provides a guiding framework for the processes required to provide training and development programmes which meet business objectives.

Summary

Training is designed to bring about a change in an individual's performance with effective training facilitating the acquisition of or a change in; *skills*, *knowledge* and *attitude* imparting a way of thinking as well as a way of doing.

A well-trained workforce will be better equipped to deal with their day-to-day activities and able to face problems and issues with confidence. Overall, well-constructed and appropriate training should lead to better and happier people in all parts of the organisation.

Training is distinct from presenting and coaching in that it involves a relatively small group people imparting new knowledge in an interactive way.

The process of training can be split into four distinct areas:

Identification

Design

Delivery

Evaluation

Each stage is important for differing reasons. The process begins with identification of learning or training needs, so in the context of training, what is identification?

IDENTIFICATION

Training Needs Analysis

Introduction

The training cycle highlights the fact that learning and development needs should first be identified before any subsequent learning and development activities are designed or delivered in fact, it is generally agreed that all training provision should be based on the accurate identification of learning needs. One of the key reasons training fails is because it is not needs based.

All too often though, the actual process of identifying training needs is undertaken in a haphazard manner, if at all.

The ability to identify training needs will greatly affect the success of any training which is subsequently delivered. Training completed which is not needs based will often have little or no positive effect.

The following chapter explores the principles of training need identification, its purpose and importance as well as considering its practical application and completion.

TRAINING NEEDS ANALYSIS

Training is generally required to rectify one of two broad situations:

- Training is required to fill a performance gap, where skills or knowledge are absent within existing business processes

- Training is required to fill a growth gap, where the need for new skills or knowledge have been brought about by changes within the organisation

A training needs analysis is undertaken with a view to identifying the specific skills and knowledge required of the learners so that they can meet their own, and ultimately the companies, business objectives.

Identifying the skills and knowledge required of the learners will facilitate the construction of training objectives. These can in turn be used to measure the effectiveness of training undertaken.

The skills gap

The process of analysing training needs it to determine what **skills or knowledge exist** and ultimately what **skills or knowledge will be required**.

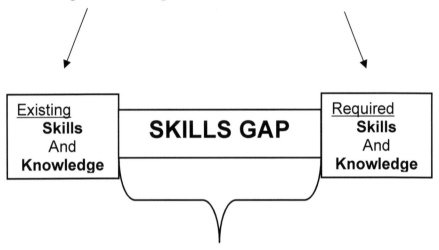

The difference between these two extremes is referred to as "**the skills gap**".

The skills or knowledge represented by this gap are the needs which the training will ultimately aim to fulfil.

Training needs analysis

Training needs analysis is often considered the building block of any training programme forming the basis for who, as well as what, will be trained. The result of the training needs analysis will form the foundation for all subsequent development activities.

Many documents may already exist which describe in detail the skills and knowledge required such as job descriptions, job specifications and role and task lists. These are often created within the organisation and updated where required and form an integral part of the training needs analysis of preparation.

Process or System Analysis

In order for the training to be effective a full understanding of the processes and systems currently in place is required.

This analysis allows the trainers to fully understand and appreciate the political, economic, social, technological, legislative and environmental factors affecting the processes and systems in place. This is not a full scale systems analysis. It is simply an information gathering technique to provide a solid background and understanding for anyone involved in the training process.

Full understanding of the systems and processes will help when training the skills and knowledge within them. Although the analysis will be focused on the system as a whole, understanding its purpose and the skills and knowledge required within it, this is also an important opportunity to gain an understanding of the forthcoming course participants. Areas for consideration are:

- Motivation
- Background
- Experience
- Skills levels
- Knowledge levels
- Participant numbers
- Geographical locations

The effectiveness of the training programme will be greatly increased with an understanding of the processes and systems however it is insight into the people issues surrounding the forthcoming training programme which will prove invaluable.

Where Job list, Job Descriptions, and Task Inventory for each job don't currently exist these may need to be created. If this information has already been compiled it is important to review and update them before moving onto the training needs analysis.

Summary

Any form of learning or training needs analysis is seeking to identify the difference between the skills and knowledge and which exist and those which are required, highlighting where gaps in skills and knowledge exist.

Filling this skills gap will ultimately be the aim of the training.

Having identified the training needs, the next step then is to design a training program which will create the required level of skills and knowledge.

DESIGNING TRAINING PROGRAMS

Designing Training Courses

Course structure

Motivating Learning

Structuring a successful training course

The 17 step training plan

Introduction

The most important aspects of the training cycle to any training professional are the design and delivery of the program.

Yes, the identification of training needs is important. One of the principal reasons training courses fail is because they are not needs based and good identification will aid course structure. Yes, it is important to measure its success by evaluating training and this will in turn lead to improvements in both design and delivery of subsequent courses. So both identification and evaluation of training are of course important however they are important because they drive the design and delivery of the training programme. The key considerations for any training programme will always be:

Does the course content hit the mark and is it well delivered.

There is no getting away from it; the design of a training course and how it is subsequently delivered will have the greatest impact on the program as a whole and therefore the training professionals' reputation and credibility.

This reputation and credibility is all important. If the training professional is employed within the company, their reputation and credibility will help when communicating and negotiating at all levels of the business. If the trainer is self-employed or working for an external company this credibility and reputation will help them maintain business levels and win further contracts.

This chapter will focus on constructing a process for training course design. It considers barriers to learning and strategies for overcoming them, assessing participant entry behaviour and setting course and session objectives. It then considers the all-important training course design offering practical steps for constructing training activities which will inspire change and motivate learning.

This chapter concludes by constructing in detail a 17 step training course plan which can be applied effectively to any training programme and used to create highly effective training courses.

Designing Training Courses

Having identified the training needs to be met by the training activity it is now necessary to design the training event.

It is important to remember the distinction between learning and training. Training is only one aspect of skill or knowledge acquisition. The specific focus here will be the design and subsequent delivery and evaluation of training activities.

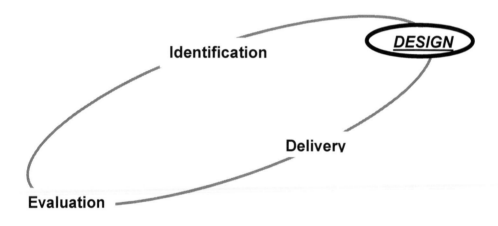

In designing a training event, the first consideration is:

"What will the participants need to know or be able to do at the conclusion of the training activity?"

In order to create effective training programmes designed to satisfy the training needs established it is important to consider:

"Why are we doing this? What do we want to achieve?"

This will alter *how* it is completed!

In other words:

First consider the required outcome and do what is required to achieve it!

Further Considerations:

The participants

Before the actual training event can be designed, thought needs to be given to the participants themselves.

What skills will they be bringing to the course?
How is their current knowledge level?
Attitudinal considerations are also required.
What are the motivation levels?
What are their aspirations?
How do they view the company?

When aware of the general level of skills, knowledge and attitude, construction of the learning activity can begin. Once constructed the final stage is to clearly define the means to be employed in order to measure the extent to which the objectives of the course have been achieved.

Barriers to learning

Whilst for many, training and development is the obvious response to skills shortages and gaps, barriers to formal training exist for many individuals. Part of the training design process involves anticipation of potential barriers to learning.

There are many barriers to learning. From an organisational perspective there may be a fear of losing staff as a result of investing time, energy and resource into their development. From the point of view of the workforce, some individuals may have a poor appreciation of the benefits of training and development or a culture where learning is not valued may exist.

Risk of losing trained staff

There is a common belief that organisations, rather than training their own staff, will simply lure trained staff away from other workplaces. As a result, some organisations still fear the repercussions of developing their own staff.

The fact is that organisations will fare better within their chosen markets if they are able to rely on well trained and motivated employees. Yes, there is a chance of losing employees after they have been trained.

It is worth remembering:

It is far better to train staff and risk losing them than to not train staff and keep them!

Culture and Attitude

One very strong barrier to learning quite common in many work environments is a culture where learning of any form is not valued. The automatic reaction of those invited to training or development activities is "why, what am I doing wrong?" In these circumstances, training has come to be viewed as a remedial activity. Only the "worst of the worst" have to suffer the humiliation of training and it is perceived very much as a punishment.

People learn constantly, generally as a result of experience. We learn in everyday activities as well as formal ones. If our previous experience is bad it will taint our future expectations and unfortunately in this situation people, sometimes entire groups of people, have experienced poor training and development practises.

If not handled correctly, this attitude will permeate through to others in the workforce and adversely affect attendance on training programmes, inhibiting the ability to attain maximum benefit from any learning activity.

Whilst this mentality has often arisen as a result of how training and development activities have been employed in the past, barriers are built which will affect future activities.

Training professionals face significant challenges where such cultures exist, however the ability to influence a destructive culture and shape it in the direction of a more positive approach to learning will reap rewards here and on future projects.

Other barriers to learning may be:

- Workload pressures
- High staff turnover
- Lack of time available
- De-motivated staff
- low staff morale
- Limited management support
- Fear of change
- Staff or management apathy

Overcoming barriers to learning

1. First determine what they are

The issues listed here can arise, forming barriers to learning and are some of the most common obstacles facing training professionals. The fact is it is not possible to overcome any barrier until the barrier is first recognised. Consider the organisation and the participants, listing the potential barriers to learning. Clarify these with further investigation prior to embarking on the learning activity.

2. Construct strategies to overcome these barriers

Having identified the potential barriers to learning, the next step is to develop strategies which will remove these barriers or at least mitigate their impact.

Beyond the practical strategies which can be employed to reduce the impact of these issues, the most important aspect in reducing these barriers is the attitude of the training team involved. Maintain a commitment to excellence and follow the steps highlighted in this book. Change people's experiences and therefore their future expectations.

The Process of Training Design

There are four areas of focus regarding the specific design of a training course or program; Define the objective of the learning event, Assess the entry behaviour of those participating in the learning event, construct and subsequently deliver the learning activity then evaluate the learning activity and amend its design where appropriate.

There is therefore, a four stage process which can be followed when designing any learning activity:

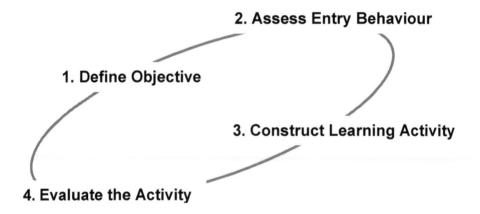

2. Assess Entry Behaviour

1. Define Objective

3. Construct Learning Activity

4. Evaluate the Activity

Whilst basic in structure, this process applies to the design of all learning activities, whether large or small, training or coaching and irrespective of its ultimate objective.

Evaluation of training activities will be covered in detail in chapter 7. Having considered how objectives can be defined and entry behaviour assessed, the remainder of this chapter will be dedicated to the all-important process of training course   design.

Assessing Entry Behaviour

Each step within this process will need to be completed however their order may well change depending on need. For example, the entry behaviour may have been assessed prior to determining the ultimate objective of the learning activity.

Assessing entry behaviour is an essential part of Training Design.

- How do the participants skill and knowledge levels compare to those required?
- What are the issues regarding language skills or reading ability?
- What other considerations are required?

Each of these aspects and more need addressing prior to construction of the training activity.

Defining Objectives

Training course objectives form the basis of effective training design. They describe the outcome of the learning in terms of the behaviour expected at the course conclusion. They state what the participants will be able to do when they have completed the objectives.

Having established what the participants will be able to do as a result of undertaking the training course, a training course is then designed which will ultimately result in them being able to do it.

The structure of course objectives is important as these offer guidance for course design and should describe exactly what will be required of both the course and those attending. They describe the outcome of the learning in terms of the expected behaviour. As such the skills, knowledge and attitude should accurately define the outcomes required of the learning.

Robert Mager provides a framework for developing objectives in his book *Preparing Instructional Objectives* (1984). His work divides the objective into three key areas:

- **Terminal Behaviour**

- **Standard of Performance**

- **Conditions of Performance**

Terminal Behaviour

The objective contains a clear statement of what the learner should be able to do at the end of the learning activity. Whether the behavioural objective is covert or overt, it should always be stated in a way that illustrates clear indicators of how the behaviour will be recognised.

This should follow the principle of being a SMART objective; that is:

S	Specific
M	Measurable
A	Achievable
R	Relevant
T	Time scaled

Specific

Specific objectives are clear and well-defined. Having clear, unambiguous objectives will help both the participant and the trainer. The participant will have a clear understanding of what is expected of them and the trainer is able to monitor and assess actual performance against the specific objectives.

Measurable

Objectives can be used as milestones with progress towards them being monitored whilst the course is under way. It is important to be able to measure the objective in order to ascertain when it has been successfully completed.

Achievable

When setting or agreeing objectives it is important to ensure that they are realistic and attainable.

Relevant

Objectives should also add useful value within the context in which they are being set, being aligned with strategies and higher business goals.

Time scaled

The objectives description should include timescales stating by when the objective must be completed. Allocating a time scale adds an appropriate sense of urgency and ensures that the objectives completion can be measured at a predetermined time.

Standard of Performance

The objective should include a clear statement of how well the participant should be able to perform the terminal behaviour. This must be measurable and so must be stated in measurable terms. These could be qualitative or quantitative or relate to time and cost.

Conditions of Performance

The objective should include a clear statement of the circumstances under which the participant should be able to perform the behaviour including any tools, equipment and information required.

Course structure

Like all good stories, a training course should have a beginning, middle and an end.

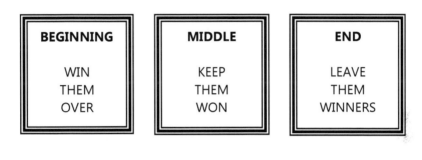

In other words:

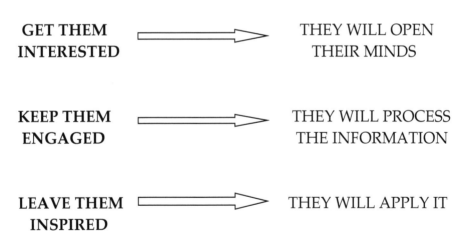

There is an old saying which is attributed to Aristotle taken from his advice for giving speeches. It has been expanded out to create a training adage which states:

> *Tell them what you're going to tell them,*
> *tell them,*
> *then tell them what you have told them.*

This forms a good basis for a good beginning, middle and an end.

Tell them what you are going to tell them
Open the course and introduce the overall objectives of the training.

Tell them
Deliver the course content

Tell them what you have told them
Close the course confirming successful attainment of the course objectives

Inspiring Change

As a training course progresses it will experience natural transitions and as such, courses should be designed to reflect this.

People tend to be territorial by their very nature. We have an inbuilt desire to create safe and secure surroundings where we feel comfortable and can relax. We seek out and create places in which we feel psychologically as well and physiologically secure in fact, our psychological and physiological well-being is intrinsically linked. This is evident as psychological stress or pressure, such as that experienced when speaking publicly creates physiological responses such as shaking hands and dry mouth. These safe mental and physical areas are often referred to as our Comfort Zones.

Anyone expanding their comfort zone, or being taken out of it all together, will experience certain physical or mental reactions. As people are removed from these areas of safety and security and placed into unusual or different situations they will experience discomfort and a feeling of being ill at ease. Their reactions are attributed to nerves and will have a significant impact on how this individual will feel and therefore behave.

With the obvious exception of training professionals, few individuals dedicate their time to undertaking training courses. As such, when they do attend a training course they may initially feel slightly uncomfortable and these feelings will invariably be manifest physically, affecting both behaviour and attitude.

It is important that Training design take this into account and incorporate activities which compensate for the natural reaction to being paced into a new or different situation.

In real terms, training is designed to stimulate learning and learning involves change. Change of skills, change in knowledge and change of attitude.

Fear of Change

Many people fear change. Actually people don't fear change, they fear *being changed*. The distinction we will explore is that of **choice**.

Anything done out of a sense of obligation is invariably hard work. It is when people feel as though they are being pushed into doing something that they push back against it. This perception of enforced change creates change resistant individuals.

Conversely, any change brought about by choice isn't even considered change. This is viewed as development.
It is important then that training is designed in such a way that all participants are encouraged to choose development rather than being forced to change.

Even if done correctly our natural desire is to return to our area of safety, to our comfort zones. That is, to go back and do what we've always done, even if this flies in the face of common sense and is obviously against our better interest. Our natural instincts don't necessarily create rational decisions. These crises of confidence may bring about feelings of uncertainty and so it is important that we reinforce the learning and reassure the learner!!

Now that the participants have acquired the skills, knowledge and attitude the training should engage hearts and minds and stimulate a desire to apply the learning and inspire action.

Motivating Learning

Win them first – win them always!

Do we want our training to be effective?
Do we want to stand out from the crowd?
Do we want to be considered one of the best at what you do?

Yes?

Then we want to move beyond simply giving information and actually inspire people to learn.

Engage the participants. Encapsulate hearts and minds.

One way to achieve this is to win the hearts and minds of those present early in the process. Open their minds. Create a desire to learn. Mind Accessing involves continuing to do so at every available opportunity.

Win them when they open their welcome pack or joining instructions. Win them with an introductory telephone call. Win them when they first walk into your training room. Win them all day and reap the benefits in your achievements, effectiveness and reputation.

Courses should be designed to encourage learning; they should be a series of wins for both the trainer and participants alike.

There are several sign-posts on the route to a well-designed training course:

- **Welcome, Introduction and orientation**
- **Gain Attention**
- **Maintain Interest**
- **Create Desire**
- **Reinforce**
- **Offer Reassurance**
- **Encourage Action and Application**

So...Beginning

Throughout the course peoples' needs will change. Before we can satisfy the needs associated with learning and development, we must first satisfy their most basic needs in line with Maslow's Hierarchy of needs.

From the course outset people have a need to feel comfortable and safe. When people are placed in a new or different situation or a position of increased stress and pressure, certain innate responses occur such as the "fight or flight" reflex. We are hard-wired with this natural response which offers protection when placed in potentially harmful situations. Course participants are fighting their natural urge to protect themselves or flee screaming! We need to take the time to demonstrate to the participants that they are in a safe environment, both physically and emotionally.

The opening part of the training session allows for introductions so that people have an idea who is around them and orientation so that they also know what is around them which helps diminish their natural "fight or flight" response. Housekeeping or ground rules will allow the trainer or the participants to establish what is or is not acceptable, behaviours which will and will not be encouraged.

As well as settling their nerves, we also need to reinforce the importance of their attendance on the course. It is at this point that the course and the trainer can grab the participant's attention, stimulate interest and motivate a desire to learn.

Interest now begins.

Middle

During the body of the course, attention and interest continue. This is now combined with strategies which will create desire. Desire for knowledge combined with a desire for its application. Engage hearts and minds and take them on a journey of success.

It is important that the trainer works hard throughout the main body of the course to offer praise and recognition. Beyond simply delivering the course content we must reinforce the learning and reassure the learners.

End

The participants have worked hard to acquire the new skills and knowledge. True learning will only occur when we see a relatively persistent change in the participant's potential behaviour as a result of this experience. It is no good simply seeing and hearing the information, they now need to use it!

The primary aim at the course conclusion is to motivate into action!

Structuring a successful training course

A successful training course will:
> **Stimulate**
> **Educate**
> **Motivate**

BEGINNING

Stimulate
- Consider the environment. We are looking to relax people and confirm that coming on the course was the right decision to make.
- Make the room as welcoming as possible.
- Have lots of natural light.
- Have music playing and drinks available.
- Greet every single participant as they enter, even if you are tied up with other things.
- Shake hands where appropriate. Begin the rapport building process and ask lots of questions.

MIDDLE

Educate
- Deliver the content in an effective and interesting way.
- Maintain a safe and comfortable environment.
- Stimulate the learner and motivate learning.

END

Motivate
- Validate the learning and encourage its application.

Course Structure:

The structure of a training course which stimulates, educates and motivates can be sub-divided into 17 key steps:

1. *Mind Accessing*
2. *Housekeeping/ground rules:*
3. *Introductions & Icebreaker*
4. *Mind Accessing*
5. *Course Objectives*
6. *Agenda*
7. *Establish Experience*
8. *Buy-in*
9. *Re-assurance*
10. *Main body*
11. *Reinforce information*
12. *Reassurance*
13. *Celebrate success*
14. *Revisit Course Objectives*
15. *Revisit Personal Objectives*
16. *Motivate into action*
17. *Course Close*

Referring back to the sign-posts of a training course, in order to stimulate, educate and motivate the course should be divided as follows:

- **Welcome, Introduction and Orientation**
- **Gain Attention**
- **Maintain Interest**
- **Create Desire**
- **Reinforce**
- **Offer reassurance**
- **Encourage Action and Application**

Combining the sign-posts and the 17 steps creates the ideal structure for an effective training course.

The 17 step training plan:

Introduction & Orientation:

1. Mind Accessing

2. Housekeeping/ground rules:

3. Introductions & Icebreaker

Gain Attention:

4. Mind Accessing

5. Course Objectives

6. Agenda

7. Establish Experience

8. Buy-in

9. Re-assurance

Maintain Interest/Create Desire:

10. Main body

Reinforce:

11. Reinforce information

Offer reassurance:

12. Reassurance

13. Celebrate success

14. Revisit Course Objectives

15. Revisit Personal Objectives

Encourage Action and Application:

16. Motivate into action

17. Course Close

The 17 step training plan in Detail

Introduction & Orientation:

1. Mind Accessing

Refer to Chapter 5, section "setting up the course"

Pre-course:

Joining Instructions:

Mind Accessing can actually begin before the course even starts.

Consider the quality of joining instructions, include directions which are easy to follow and describe the course objectives and content. Allow people to feel comfortable about attending.

Introductory telephone call:

Take the time to make an introductory telephone call to each participant. This will help to relax the participants, getting them on-side and goes a long way to relaxing you as the trainer.

On arrival:

Refer to Chapter 5, section "Creating the right environment"

Create a welcoming environment.
Have music playing

Introduce and shake hands
Display Motivational quotes/statements on posters/pictures around the room or revolving on a PowerPoint presentation

2. Housekeeping/ground rules:

Housekeeping:

With a view to confirming the participants safety and comfort, run through some general housekeeping.

Examples:

- Need to sign in/out
- Smoking
- Meals
- Breaks
- Fire drills/Fire Precautions
- Facilities e.g. toilets

Ground rules:

Either give or agree ground rules which highlight the rights and responsibilities of all present (including the trainer who has rights too!)

Example areas:

- Punctuality
- Language
- Interrupting ("one singer, one song")
- Involvement
- Participation

3. Introductions & Icebreaker

Refer to Chapter 9, section "Icebreakers & Introductions"

Gain Attention:

4. Mind Accessing

Refer to Chapter 9, section "Mind Accessing Attention grabbers"

The use of a short story, anecdote or quote which can be linked to the learning to participants will allow people to breakdown some of their barriers to learning and make them more receptive to the forthcoming ideas, concepts or theories to be introduced.

5. Course Objectives

Refer to Chapter 4, section "Constructing objectives"

Where possible present the course or session objectives using PowerPoint or any media which will present directly onto a screen or wall. Ensure the presentation can build the bullet points. Any information displayed on the screen will be read immediately so ensure each objective builds separately.

Ask a different participant to read each of the objectives. This has several advantages. It gains interaction early on in the course and facilitates participant buy-in. This also relieves some of the pressure often felt early in the course and allows the trainer to take a quick deep breath and compose themselves if required.

Leave the objectives on the screen as you move on to reveal the agenda.

6. Agenda

The agenda should be presented on a flipchart where available. This offers a mix of media early in the course following the use of PowerPoint which was used for the objectives, it also allows for several advantages to be enjoyed.

Firstly, this allows for the objectives to remain in view while the agenda is presented.

Secondly, the flipchart page can be posted on the wall. This can be seen and therefore used as a prompt by the trainer, offering a sign-post for the session or day.

The participants can also use it to see where they are at any part of the day. Agenda points can be ticked off as they are completed offering the opportunity to celebrate success

7. Establish Experience

The effectiveness of your training will be greatly increased with your ability to create and maintain rapport (*Refer to Chapter 6, section "Rapport"*). Most people, when they are getting on well, will be in a state of unconscious rapport. They are more amenable, receptive and open to new ideas and concepts so it is important to enhance the rapport building process at every available opportunity.

Rapport is a perceived affinity between two or more people.

As human beings we have certain basic physiological and psychological needs which make human behaviour very simple to predict. People love talking; they adore talking about themselves and by this point of the course people are both ready and more importantly willing to talk, especially about themselves.

Rapport building entails establishing common ground. What do you have in common? Well, at this point their attendance on a training course. Encourage them to share their experience, talking about their experience of courses and about themselves generally. This has two benefits. Firstly it gets the participants talking which relaxes both them and you and secondly allows an insight into their previous experiences of the subject matter and of training, whether good or bad.

8. Buy-in

Before entering in to the main body of the session it is important to gain the buy-in of the participants. Establish a reason for the participants to pay attention, and give them a reason to listen. Gain commitment to their full participation.

One method of establishing participant buy-in is to encourage the construction of personal objectives. The advantage of having the course/session objectives displayed on-screen and the agenda displayed on a Flipchart means that the participants are picking up cues regarding their own objectives.

When completed at this point and in this way, personal objectives will invariably mirror those of the course or session.

Personal Objectives:

The method of recording personal objectives will vary depending on the course structure and time available.

Recording Personal Objectives on flip-chart

If the Personal Objectives are to be recorded on the Flipchart, ensure the Agenda sheet is first posted to the wall.

Having viewed what you expect them to be able to achieve by the end of the course or session - the objectives, and viewed how this will be achieved – the agenda, ask the participants to consider what they would like to take from the course.

Allow a small amount of time to think about and construct their own objectives. Go round the group and record each on the flip chart.

Positives:

Good practise
Allows repetition of key themes
Formally recorded
Can be posted on wall for participants to refer to, which maintains focus
When posted, forms a reminder of participant's names
Allows trainer to control input if required
Allows trainer to manage expectations

Draw-backs:

May be time consuming
May appear repetitive if not controlled

Recording Personal Objectives on Post-it notes

This follows similar practise however the participants record their own objectives, one per post-it. These are them placed up on a flip chart to be referred back to later.

Positives:

Also good practise
Formally recorded
Can be posted on wall for participants to refer to, which maintains focus
Can still be posted under individual names
Requires less time
Can still be read out to repeat key themes

Draw-backs:

Less easy to control content
Objectives may be less clear

It is important to note that if a personal objective is raised which will not be achieved on the course, confirm this at this point. It is important to manage expectations.

9. Re-assurance

As a final stage before entering into the core course content, it is important to set the participants minds at rest. Explain how the information will be introduced or delivered. The core course content will be offered in a logical way which the participants should find easy to follow.

Encourage questions. Explain that if the participants don't understand that is the fault of the training, not theirs.

Use a session introducer to engage the participants. A good example would be Baden Powell's quote, see Mind Accessing Attention grabbers.

Maintain Interest/Create Desire:

10. Main body

The main body of the training course should follow a logical flow and structure. Information should be introduced in a manner which aids learning and facilitates memory.

The course flow and structure should introduce information, ideas and concepts in an order which makes the information easy to remember and also use, (*Refer to Chapter 5, section "Delivering Training Programmes"*). Learning information in the order in which it will be employed encourages a logical flow and facilitates its ultimate use.

Account for the manner in which different people learn, (*Refer to Chapter 1, sections on "Learning".* Encourage participation.

Allow time for and encourage reflection and the development or practical application of abstract ideas and concepts.

Use a mix of delivery methods and styles. Facilitate multi-sensory learning.

Allow plenty of breaks.

Reinforce:

11. Reinforce information

Repetition is the mother of all learning. The key is to repeat, repeat and repeat again without appearing repetitive! *(Refer to Chapter 5, section "Repetition").*

Start each day with a review of the previous day's content. Use different exercises to keep this fresh and interesting. Close each session with reference to the objectives and a summary of the session content.

Encourage exercises which stimulate thought. Use stories and anecdotes to reinforce key concepts.

Employ Key Point Checks and session Validation exercises.

Offer reassurance:

12. Reassurance

Psychological approaches to learning confirm the innate desire to return to the norm. To go back and do what we have always done. The manner in which the human brain is programmed results in existing skills and knowledge being "un-learned" in order for them to be replaced or enhanced by the new skills and knowledge being studied. Without reassurance in some part, this desire to reject the new learning may loom large in a participants mind.

This reassurance may be as simple as reinforcing the need for new procedures or emphasising the benefits experienced by former participants who have employed the new skills or knowledge.

13. Celebrate success

Part of the reassurance process involves stepping out of the learning loop and celebrating the success attained so far. People are generally motivated to some extent by praise and enjoy the satisfaction derived from accomplishment.

Reinforce just how much the participants have achieved and how far they have come since initially joining the course.

14. Revisit Course Objectives

One method of celebrating success is to review the course objectives. This offers a conclusion to the learning, reinforces the success of the course and more importantly the participants and rewards the effort involved.

15. Revisit Personal Objectives

To further celebrate success and maintain participant buy-in, reviewing the participants personal objectives will reassure those present, further reward their effort and reinforce the positive impact of attending the course.

Encourage Action and Application:

16. Motivate into action

There is an old, well known and well used saying:

KNOWLEDGE IS POWER

Actually from a training point of view:

APPLIED KNOWLEDGE IS **MORE POWERFULL**!!

Simply having new skills and knowledge does not aid success. They are only of benefit if they are used. Successful training courses and successful trainers motivate their participants into action, stimulating use of the skills and knowledge learned. This has a multiplying effect. As the learned skills and knowledge are employed results will begin to change. People will notice changes in behaviour.

The impact of the training will be recognised if the output of the training is employed. This will lead to greater results and further demands for training and development.

17. Course Close

It is important that the participants leave the course on a high. This has many positive benefits:

Firstly, if people feel good about themselves they will feel better about the new skills and knowledge. If they feel better about themselves and their new abilities, they are more inclined to use them.

It would be great if everybody in life was positive and offered whole-hearted support to their colleagues and the success of others. Unfortunately however, the world is full of people who believe that the only way to look good is to make other people look bad.

This may well be the attitude facing our participants on their return to work or life in general. Others, who have not undergone training, may wish to maintain the status quo, to keep things the same. It would be ideal if the participants returned, began outperforming those around them and those others recognised the positive benefits of the improvement and either attended the training or worked hard to develop their own skills. That would be the ideal. Unfortunately what actually often happens is that these other workers, employees or colleagues seek to drag the participants back to their level.

They will either begin on the offensive with statements such as "Okay, now back in the real world…." or "That's not how things work around here…." or "I've been here longer than you. These new fads have come and gone. They never work…." These statements cast doubts in the participant's minds and affect their ability to employ the new skills, or stop them even trying.

Alternatively these people will wait their time. They will watch carefully, choosing to ignore any successes and leap on the slightest failure when the new learning is initially employed, encouraging a return to "how things *really* work around here…"

Our course close should inspire the participants and motivate to action. It should also offer resilience against negativity and initial issues encountered when trying to employ the new learning.

Secondly, if the participants leave on a high they will discuss attendance on the programme in a positive way which will encourage further attendance by others and break down barriers to learning these others may experience. The participants will be more ready to attend subsequent learning and should join with a far better attitude to learning.

The reputation of the training programme has a great impact of the reputation of those training it.

Summary

The importance of good training course design cannot be over emphasised. A well-structured training course will help the training activity meet its own objectives and satisfy the needs of its participants. Many barriers to learning can be broken down by good course design and a well-structured training programme.

A well-designed and well-structured training course will motivate learning. It will encourage personal development and stimulates change, a change of skills a change of knowledge and perhaps even a change of attitude.

There are several signposts on the route to a well-designed training course:

- Welcome, Introduction and Orientation
- Gain Attention
- Maintain Interest
- Create Desire
- Reinforce
- Offer Reassurance
- Encourage Action and Application

The 17 step training plan can be applied to any training programme to create highly effective and successful training courses.

A well-structured, well designed training course will **stimulate**, **educate** and **motivate**.

One of the major factors affecting its success is how the training is subsequently delivered.

DELIVERING TRAINING PROGRAMS

Mind Accessing

Setting up the course

Creating the right environment

Dealing with the fear of public speaking

Gaining and maintaining participation (questioning)

The power of yes

Praise and Recognition

Repetition is the mother of all learning

Giving feedback

Working the group

How to deal with reluctant learners

Closing the course

Introduction

Having designed a well-structured, stimulating, educational training course, the most important aspect of training begins – its delivery.

Training course delivery is the most important aspect of the overall training process because it is the most visible. Every aspect of a training course will be scrutinised and judged however none more so than the manner in which it is delivered.

The need for credibility

Whether it be because of a bad past experience or no experience at all, from receipt of the joining instructions many prospective participants will experience some nerves. Attending a training course can be quite daunting.

Whilst on the course they will be expected to actively participate in sessions, group discussion, syndicate exercises and perhaps role-plays. They will be expected to meet a certain, predetermined standard and they will be encouraged to do that which often creates the most resistance, they will be encouraged to change. Change skills, change knowledge or even change their attitude.

If participants are to approach this course with a positive frame of mind, immerse themselves fully in the learning experience and gain maximum benefit from the opportunity they need to have total faith, trust and confidence in the training professional running the program.

The trainer's credibility is all important and it will be measured based on how the training program is delivered from the receipt of the joining pack to the venue, size and layout of the training room, the quality of the facilities and ultimately the session delivery.

Many participants arrive on a training course with pre-built barriers to learning. All aspects of training course delivery from an introductory telephone call, creating the right training environment the trainer's ability to worked with the group and stimulate and maintain interest can be used to gradually chip away at these barriers, gaining the participants buy-in and enhance their learning experience.

The following chapter focuses all aspects of training course delivery offering simple, practical steps which can be applied to enhance a training course, workshop or even presentation.

Delivering Training Programs

Having correctly identified the training need and design a program which will fills the skills gaps identified, the next stage of the process is to deliver the training program.

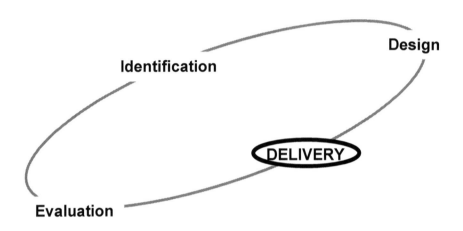

Whilst the entire training cycle is important, with identification leading to course design and evaluation reconfirming its success or leading to further development, the most important part of the entire learning and development process is delivery of the program.

The manner in which the program is delivered will determine the success of its output and ultimately impact on the skills learned being employed.

From setting up the course and creating the right environment to the actual style in which the content is to be delivered. Creating and maintaining participation, reinforcing the content and then working the group. Use positive communication skills and active listening techniques and dealing with reluctant learners.

All of these things will affect the success of the course. The way in which the course is received will not only affect the result of the course, it will impact on the demand for further learning and development activities.

Mind Accessing

The mind is like a parachute – it works best when it is open.

One of the principle barriers to learning is attitude. If people don't want to learn they rarely will. Without recognising the benefit of learning, people will rarely want to learn.

Mind accessing refers to the process of opening people's minds, the process of removing, or at least reducing potential barriers to learning.

Mind accessing involves opening people's minds to new theories, concepts or ideas, prior to their introduction.

For Example

An individual is told they are to attend a three-day training course. Whilst from a training point of view we would want to believe that they will wholeheartedly support their inclusion on the course and wait with eager anticipation of its beginning, we know that very often the reality is something different.

Firstly, the forthcoming attendee may wonder why they have been included.

What am I doing wrong that warrants my attendance on a training course?

Secondly the human brain tends to work by association so their next reaction may be to compare this news to their previous experience.

If they have never been on a training course, fear and apprehension may begin to surface in the individual's mind:

What will they ask me to do?
I'm not joining in; they aren't making me look like a fool!

If they have attended a course where these issues were not addressed first time around, they may continue:

I remember the last time. They made me do that role-play. I'll never fall for that again.

I remember giving an answer and the trainer said I was wrong, right in front of everyone, I'll not get caught like that again!

What a waste of time.

As previously discussed,

P = R, not the truth

Perception is reality, not necessarily the truth.

While ever the attendees have these thoughts and feel this way, it will affect their attitude when they arrive on the course.

Perceptions based on apprehension create fear which manifests itself in barriers to learning.

Whilst these perceptions may not be true in reality, they are true to the participants until they have been convinced otherwise. These attitudes create the barriers to learning so prevalent within training courses.

Open their minds

Mind Accessing involves subtle techniques which are employed in order to chip away at these perceptions, set the participants mind at rest, break down barriers to learning and open minds to the new ideas, concepts and theories to be introduced.

Participants with an **open mind** are more inclined to *listen*.

If they then **believe** it they will then *apply* the learning.

It is this difference between really good, effective training and the run-of-the-mill training or teaching these participants may have experienced previously.

When to open minds

It is important to open minds early in the training process and then to continue this throughout. Always open minds before introducing new ideas and concepts. Opening minds towards the end of the course will allow the participants to leave believing the importance of applying the new learning.

Pre-Course

Mind Accessing can begin before the course actually starts.

Whilst people are information gatherers by their very nature, they are often selective in the information they seek out. People actually seek out information which reinforces their view of the world. If their opinion of training is poor, they will actively seek out information which confirms this perception.

Refer to the following section in this book "Setting up the course". The quality and accuracy of joining material goes a long way to breaking down these barriers right from the fore.

An introductory telephone call will help break-down these barriers by allowing the trainer to introduce themselves and answer any fears or queries before the course has even begun.

On Arrival

If the participant's perception of training is of a sterile course atmosphere where their opinion counts for nothing and they are going to be told what to think, say and do – change their perception.

Refer to the section "Creating the right environment" which follows shortly. Create a warm and welcoming atmosphere. Access the participant's minds on all channels, visual, auditory and kinaesthetic (emotional) level. Play music and offer an introduction to each participant as they enter. Post motivational sayings and phrases around the walls.

During the course

Effective training promotes change. Rather than thinking of training as a form of education, where information is given, help people to learn. Use stories and anecdotes to introduce new ideas and concepts.

The power of a message is in its delivery

Stories can be used to gain the participants attention and then maintain interest. They can create and reinforce a need or desire and offer reassurance.

Use the participant's physiology. When trying to change mind sets, change physiology. Consider when to use exercises or session shakers and get them out of their seats. Changing physiology changes minds.

Following are examples of stories and anecdotes which can be used as Mind Accessing tools, link the learning to the participants experience and break down barriers to learning.

Example of Anecdote for Sales Training

Selling should be straightforward and rather surprisingly, is generally only overcomplicated by those trying to do it.

The best way to view selling is as a "Buying Process". Realistically how many people truly enjoy being "sold" to? How many of us would go into work and say "I had a great day yesterday, I went into a motor dealership and someone sold me a car"?

What we would actually say is "I *bought* a car".

There is a distinct difference between buying and being sold to. That difference is the perception of control. If you build sufficient value in any product or service, the customer will want to buy it. It's not up to the salesperson to force the customer to do anything; they should *want* to take it.

From a training point of view we are trying to get the "buy in" of the participants rather than "sell them" on the concept – if you'll excuse the pun!

The following is a way of conveying this concept during a training course.

A young Salesperson was disappointed as he had lost an important sale. In discussing the matter with his Sales Manager, the young man shrugged.

"I guess," he said "it just proves you can lead a horse to water, you can't make him drink."

"Son," said the Sales Manager, "let me give you a piece of advice: your job is not to make him drink. It's to make him thirsty."

Example of Anecdote for Expertise

It is generally accepted that those who have achieved expertise in a particular field command higher salaries. When training it will prove beneficial to reinforce this fact and encourage a positive approach to learning:

> Production plants employ hundreds of people. These plants often work to incredibly tight timescales. The mass produced nature of their work means that if one area of the production line ceases to work, production from an entire line will be held up. These lines invariably employ massive, incredibly complicated machinery.
>
> One such plant encountered a serious problem. Production from one of the primary machines had ground to a halt. An outside consultant was brought into repair it.
>
> The consultant looked the machine up and down. He drew a small rubber mallet out of an old brown work-bag. He walked slowly along the machine resting his left hand lightly on his it's surface, his face mere millimetres away, listening intently. Eventually he stops, takes a step back and offers several light taps with the mallet. The machine groans back into life.
>
> An invoice is left requiring payment of £2000. The manager who had requested the services of the workman was shocked and insisted on a breakdown of the Invoice.

The serviceman was happy to oblige. The breakdown read:

For hitting the machine –   Fee £50
For knowing where to hit the machine –   Fee £1950

Setting up the course

Vanilla is still the favourite flavour - First get the basics right!

Leading restaurateurs confirm that even with the plethora of flavours now available, vanilla remains the most popular. It is important to get this one right before providing any of the more complicated combinations of flavours.

This simple analogy can be transferred to all aspects of business, most notably setting up training courses. First, get the basics right.

This is probably the first contact we will have with the participants so it is imperative that it is good. Everything they see, hear, taste, touch and smell should be perfect!

Joining instructions

Joining instructions play a key role in course set-up. They are invariably the first communication the participants will receive and are important for many reasons.

The participants will be nervous. Their apprehensions may be reduced by the receipt of joining instructions offering a good indication of what will be expected of them.

The joining instructions offer clear guidelines for attendance on the course. They should be designed to eliminate the embarrassment of arriving late or ill-prepared.

The quality of the joining instruction can begin the process of mind-accessing. High quality, accurate and welcoming joining instructions can begin to settle the participants into a learning frame of mind.

As well as offering a warm welcome they should contain details regarding:

- Time
- Date
- Venue
- Dress-code
- Trainers' names and contact details

Where available a course timetable and details of the course objectives can be included.
The joining instructions should detail any items the participants are required to bring with them to the course. They can also deliver pre-course requirements, that is, details of any pre-course work or exercises which require completion.

Introductory telephone call

Having received the joining instructions the participants will feel more at ease and fully understand all which is required of them in preparation for the course.

A further step is to contact each participant individually by telephone in anticipation of attending the course. The call allows the trainer the opportunity to introduce themselves, outline the first day and answer any questions the participant may have.

The benefits received from making these calls will far out way the time required to complete them.

Firstly the call allows the trainer to confirm all areas of the joining instructions. This, in turn, allows the participants to ask any questions which may have arisen as a result of receiving the joining instructions or about the course generally and further allay any fears before they arrive on the day.

The call also allows each party to put a "voice to the name". The participant will arrive on the course feeling that they know at least one other person and the trainer will have begun the all-important process of rapport building. This call begins to break down barriers to learning before the course has even begun. If there are any issues it is far better to handle them by phone and in private rather than on the first day and in public.

Creating the right environment

During the now almost legendary talks between Ronald Reagan and Mikhail Gorbachev, the pair had reached an impasse and the negotiations stalled. Reagan invited Mr Gorbachev to join him for walk in the gardens. It is said that on their return the treaty was signed. With the change of environment came a change of focus, attention and most importantly attitude.

Influencing change:

An incredibly powerful tool for changing your own or someone else's behaviour can be accomplished by first changing the environment. If you can control the environment you can typically predict or create a specific behaviour.

Creating the right environment

Most people attending a training course will be nervous, irrespective of whether or not they actually want to be there on the day. It is crucial that we break down barriers and relax those attending this learning experience as quickly as possible if it is to have maximum effect.

Unless relaxed, the participants of training courses will not be open to any new theories or concepts and, very much like children, participants of training courses need to feel safe and comfortable if they are to be truly relaxed.

All actions which we undertake, from the very first introductory telephone call or letter through to how we close the course on the final day should be geared around enhancing and maximising the impact of our learning solution. One significant aspect of the overall experience over which we should take complete control is the training room in which the experienced will take place.

Anyone who has conducted research or reading in the area of motivation will probably be aware of the work of Maslow and Hertzberg, to name a few. In examining each of these theories of motivation it is possible to see a general trend establishing.

Maslow discusses a hierarchy of needs. The lowest need must first be satisfied in order for subsequent needs to be met. So, physiological needs require consideration and must be satisfied before any work on subsequent needs will have any impact. We must then focus on the safety needs of the participants, before work on the more motivating aspects will have any effect.

We must therefore consider the physiological and safety needs important to participants.

Hertzberg also explains that "hygiene factors" require satisfying before motivating factors will take effect.

Both Hertzberg and Maslow recognise that unless the very basic needs are met, the impact of subsequent attempts to motivate will be greatly reduced, if not negated totally. It is evident from these studies that before any high-level motivation can occur we must first satisfy the most basic of needs.

So what are the most basic needs from a training perspective?

Well, as previously mentioned, the first exposure the participants will have to our training will be via our introductory communications and so all these must be well organised and of the highest quality.

We, however, must first consider the venue.

The training venue

Access:

Access to the venue is of paramount importance both for the trainer and of course, the participants.

Consider the type of venue available. There are many dedicated training sites or hotels who offer specific training facilities however it is rewarding to think beyond the norm.

Other venues which are becoming more popular are sports grounds and racetracks, both for horses and motorsport. These often provide excellent training facilities and will often include a tour of the ground or track at no additional cost. Anything which differentiates your course from the "norm" may have a positive impact.

Trainer access

The room must be set up and all preparation completed prior to arrival by any of the participants. As a result, it is important to be able to gain entry to the facilities at least one hour before the first expected arrival.

Participant access

If participants are travelling to the venue then there should be easy links to public transport as well as adequate parking facilities. An increasing number of hotels now charge for parking. If any additional cost is to be borne by the participants, this must be included in the joining packs.

Confirm the room's access ability, including for those with limited mobility.

Appearance:

The course as a whole will be judged partly on where it is held. The look and feel of the venue should provide a mixture of professionalism and comfort. All aspects of the facilities should be clean, well-kept and well presented. Attention to detail should be maintained by all aspects of the facilities, including the attitude of the staff.

Facilities:

If the course is to be residential, additional facilities such as swimming pool, gymnasium and other recreational facilities will prove an important and well-received addition to the course.

Check availability of sockets. Arrange for an extension cable if required.

Confirm availability of flip charts, flip chart paper, pens, flip chart pens, pencils and paper. If these are to be charged at an additional cost it may be worth providing these yourself.

The Training Room

Size:

Arrange for a room which is sufficiently large enough to accommodate the numbers you are expecting for your training course. This is different to the size of room required if you're running a meeting. In a meeting, one table in the centre of the room will be sufficient and people can sit on each side, forming a rectangle.

In a training environment, at least one side of the rectangle must be left open so that all present can see the front of the room, facilitating the use of flip charts, laptop projector and screen. This significantly changes the size of room required.

Room arrangement:

Allow time to arrange the furniture and articles within the room exactly how you would like it. If required, ask for member of staff to help.

Furniture:

The participants of your training course will be sat in chairs for a significant portion of the day so ensure they are comfortable. Also, ensure that all the furniture in the room match and are not damaged, the aesthetics of the room are incredibly important. If the room looks appealing it will help break down barriers and relax the participants.

Arrange for a table to be available at the front of the room, set to one side which you can use for your materials and equipment.

If required, check the screen for any marks, or damage. Participants lean on their tables, knock them when they move and may shake them when they speak so arrange for a separate table to be placed at the front of the room to accommodate the projector.

Don't allow too much space between the table from which you will be presenting and the participants. Reducing the amount of space between you and the learners will help increase the effectiveness of the training session. Closing the distance between you and the learner is both physically and emotionally will help the participants feel better about you, themselves and the training sessions a whole.

Availability of natural light:

Natural light is incredibly powerful. It is uplifting and helps maintain attention and interest levels. Confirm that the room has windows and so access to natural light. If the room has windows down one side confirm that this is not directly facing the sun as on a hot day this will make any attempt to control the room temperature almost impossible and provide for a very uncomfortable training environment. Consider the effect the light will have on any screen you may be using. Ensure that you can control access to this light.

Snacks and drinks:

Check the availability of tea and coffee making facilities.

If bottled water, sweets, biscuits and fruit are not provided, then provide your own. It is incredible the effect such simple creature comforts can have on the participants collective or individual attitude. Providing sweets, biscuits and fruit are relatively inexpensive yet have a significant impact.

Breakout areas:

Consider the quality and quantity of breakout areas available, whether they be the reception area, communal coffee areas or if weather permits, the gardens.

If required, book separate breakout rooms. Ensure these are close to the main training area and check their size and cleanliness before using them.

Air-conditioning:

As soon as you have more than one person in the room it is very difficult to please all of the people all the time. At least if the room is air-conditioned and you have control of it, you can try. Maintain control of the room temperature yourself. If a participant adjusts the temperature of the room, they will do so to extremes. If they feel slightly too cold they will create a significant increase in the room's temperature which will have a detrimental effect on everyone else's ability to concentrate as the room gets warmer. When adjusting the air-conditioning unit make changes one or two degrees at a time and allow the unit time to work.

Equipment:

Ensure that flip charts have sufficient paper and that pens are available. Check quickly through the flip chart pads to ensure that all the pages are clean and have not yet been written on. Write a welcome message on the top page.

Setup and check your projector. Ensure the image fills the screen with no overlap and that the image is level and square. It is very frustrating to sit in any session where the visual equipment has not been set up correctly.

Check any other audio-visual equipment you will be using such as televisions, DVD or audio players. If you're using any form of camera equipment check this before the session begins.

Participant equipment

Ensure each participant has clear and clean notepaper and a working pen. Lay them out neatly where you want each of the participants to sit. Leave them post it notes and a name card if these are to be used.

Place articles which can be used as "stress" balls. Ensure they are light, made of foam rubber or a similar substance.

Ambience:

Finally, and in preparation for the arrival of the participants, have some music playing. People rarely like quiet rooms and feel more comfortable entering a room which already has music playing. Having pleasant music playing in the room will create a more relaxed atmosphere and people will be more likely to begin talking if there is some form of noise, such as music, already in the room. As an example, people soon stop talking in church once the organ music ends!

Dealing with the fear of public speaking

Fear is the darkroom where negatives are developed

It seems extraordinary that anyone with a fear of public speaking would seek to perform the role of a trainer or facilitator yet there are many such brave souls out there. They grasp the nettle on a daily basis, overcoming incredible fear and help people learn. Many would learn simply by knowing this fact. I have worked with one such individual who was violently ill before the start of each day's sessions.

I remember confronting him about this and asking how he got through it. He explained that he knew that there were many people who cared for him and he looked forward to telling them how well the training had gone.

He saw his role as being very important and recognise the value he had in other people's lives. This realisation and his own personal pride carried him through each day and he relished the opportunity to share his successors with those who were dear to him.

Training can be an odd profession. Whilst you very often forge incredibly close relationships and friendships, they are often short-lived, so you are constantly surrounded by new people.

As a result Training can be a very lonely job. It just doesn't very often feel like it as you are constantly surrounded by people - quite the dichotomy.

This isolation very often leads to apprehension and fear sometimes creeps in. Demons are unleashed, those demons which turn the nicest participants into difficult delegates before they have even spoken a word and makes the most positive of groups cold and un-co-operative before they have even arrived.

Sometimes we actually have difficult participants and groups who are cold and un-co-operative and so the isolation can increase.

So how do the people successfully overcome the fear of public speaking?

They recognise that these fears are purely demons and rarely real. These fears are just fears and are far bigger in their head and heart. They will be forgotten tomorrow, although more likely later today.

Always remember that:

Whenever you're lonely remember it's true
Somewhere there's someone who's thinking of you.

There may be one or more people for whom you go out to work each day. People who you care for and who care for you. People who rely on you. It may simply be yourself, it could be a wife or husband, mother or father, sibling or friend.

Just remember that this is a course which will live in your memory as the success that you make it.

For now, think of those loved ones and imagine yourself describing how well the course went. They want you to succeed. Create your own self-fulfilling prophecy.

Where fear becomes a reality

There are certain unavoidable physiological responses which any form of public speaking will generally create:

- Blushing
- Sweating
- Feeling of sickness
- Clammy palms
- Knocking knees
- Dry mouth
- Blank mind
- Shaking hands
- Self-doubt
- And a need to "get out of here!"

Conquering training nerves

First of all, it is important to acknowledge the fact that most of these will happen on almost every training course to some degree or other. All trainers experience nerves on some level, it's just that the good ones have learned to work with their nerves rather than allowing their nerves to work against them.

Nerves are good, they prove that we are still alive! They also act as a warning mechanism. You cannot remove nerves, to some degree, they will always be there.

Accepting the fact that nerves exist allows us to input strategies which will mitigate their effects.

Blushing

Blushing tends to increase in line with discomfort of some form and is often associated with a drop in confidence however the biggest cause for blushing is the fear of blushing!

Winston Churchill famously said "When I look back on all these worries, I remember the story of the old man who said on his deathbed that he had had a lot of trouble in his life, most of which had never happened."

As with most fears in life, once we accept the fact that they may happen they often don't. The following strategies will help increase confidence and reduce this fear.

Sweating

There is little which can be done to actually stop sweating so it is important to disguise it. On the first day of any training course wear a white shirt/blouse. Any form of perspiration will appear less obvious.

Manage the temperature in the room.

Try not to worry about it. Remember, as confidence increases, nerves and perspiration decrease.

Feeling of sickness

That feeling of sickness is simply adrenaline coursing through the body as the part of the brain which preaches common sense screams "get out". This happens in response to our nerves and the body getting ready to run. It is also why our palms go clammy, our knees and hands shake slightly and our mouth goes dry.

Take some deep breaths, relax and remember what is truly important in life.

The participants are more nervous than the trainer, they just don't show it.

Have a glass or bottle of water to hand, this will help settle a nervous stomach and dry mouth.

Having a glass of water available also helps on those rare occasions when the mind goes blank. What the mind actually needs is a second or two to compose itself and move onto the next section. Unfortunately one or two seconds in front of 15 people seems like an eternity so take a couple of sips of water to fill the dead space. Those present will not realise what is happening.

Hands which shake are only noticeable if they are holding a piece of paper, a cup and saucer or maracas so put them down!

Universal techniques for mitigating training nerves

Know the subject

One of the main contributors to nerves is self-doubt. Know the subject-matter and more importantly, be confident in your knowledge of the subject matter. You know more than the participants.

Practise

Amateurs practise until they get it right. Professionals practise until they can't get it wrong.

Practise, practise and practise again. The more confident you are in your ability to deliver the material flawlessly, the more confident you are.

Introductory telephone call

Take the time to make an introductory telephone call to each of the participants. Settle their nerves and ensure they are perfectly happy with the joining instructions, directions etc.

This has the dual advantage of relaxing both the participants, getting them on-side before the course even begins and relaxing you as the trainer.

The participants will not be strangers when they arrive and barriers to training are already being broken down.

Check the room set up

The biggest asset available to any trainer looking to quell nerves is time.

Invariably training venues, including our own, strive to offer first-class service. With the best will in the world though the setup is unlikely to be exactly how we would want it.

Lack of time creates nerves. Ensure access is available at least one hour before the participant's estimated earliest arrival and turn up 15 minutes before that in case the person with the keys isn't available!

Set up the room to your liking with no compromise.

Check the equipment

Another aspect of training delivery which sets nerves jangling is the fear that things will go wrong so, do all you can to ensure that everything goes right.

In the hit series the "X – files", Fox Moulder one of the main protagonists had a very appropriate password for his computer sign in. He used "TRUST NO1". This could be read as trust number one i.e. trust yourself or trust no one i.e. trust no one other than yourself, either version works!

Yes, it sounds awful, "trust no one", after all we are generally surrounded by really nice, helpful people. It is worth remembering however they are not the one stood in front of 15 participants with a projector that doesn't work properly!

Check the projector. Use the keystone feature to ensure a perfectly square image on the screen (with no overlap). Run all presentations at least once.

Ensure the flip chart has plenty of clean paper on which nobody has already written. Make sure there are sufficient flip chart marker pens and that they work.

Test everything. Test the appliances, test them again and, just for good measure, test them one last time. Leave nothing to chance.

Divert attention briefly

Nerves increase in the first few minutes so allow the opportunity to take a deep breath and compose yourself. In the first few minutes, use a prepared flip chart message, PowerPoint slide or brief prepared presentation to divert attention away from yourself for a couple of seconds. Take a couple of deep breaths and compose yourself.

Get the monkey off your back!

A trainer will get nervous early on in a training course if they are the one doing all the talking. Figuratively get the monkey off your back and pass it to the participants. Engage them briefly in some way whether it be with personal introductions, an icebreaker, an exercise or simply by eliciting their opinion.

Housekeeping/ground rules

Often the reaction of nervous participants can add to the nerves of a trainer. Work with the dissidents to establish housekeeping and/or ground rules setting the minds of the participants and the trainer at rest. Head them off at the pass from a training perspective.

Be comfortable with the environment

We end with the most powerful way to overcome nerves in any form of public speaking:

> ## *Walk the room!!!*

Familiarise yourself with the environment. Before the participants arrive walk around the room. Allow plenty of time to include this as part of the initial preparations. Walk the room several times and in all directions. Have a good look around and get comfortable with where everything is, with the look and feel.

Why?

Whenever we expand our comfort zones, or leap outside them, there is an innate psychological desire to run away. This is mistakenly perceived as a desire to run away from the cause of our nerves or apprehension. It is actually a desire to return to where we feel safe, to return to our comfort zone.

In walking the room we are going a long way towards creating a new area in which we feel comfortable, we are beginning to create a new comfort zone.

Our instincts are known as "first nature", that is, the things with which we are born as opposed to those which we learn. One of our instincts is that of "fight or flight". When we are placed in a situation of high stress our automatic response is to either stand and fight or run away. It is an inbuilt safety mechanism left over from the time when we were both predator and prey. If we do not walk the room, if we do not make ourselves feel a modicum of comfort in this situation, when we enter it in preparation for any form of public speaking, especially some form of training activity we will create this fight or flight response.

Allow yourself to feel comfortable in the room before anybody else arrives.

Gaining and maintaining participation

Questioning

A question is more powerful than a statement

If you tell somebody something, they may well believe you. If the individual comes to their own conclusion then the fact becomes almost indisputable within their own mind.

So, how do you get people to come to their own conclusions? You ask them questions. The questions you ask therefore become incredibly important as it is these which will direct them towards their conclusion.

People would rather be challenged than told

Much has been written on the subject of questioning within an educational context, many begin by invoking Socrates. Socrates was a famous Athenian teacher who seldom directly told his pupils anything. The Socratic method of using questions and answers to challenge assumptions, expose contradictions, and lead to new knowledge and wisdom is an undeniably powerful training approach.

In addition to its long history and demonstrated effectiveness, questioning is also of interest because of its widespread use as a contemporary educational technique.

So, what is a question?

A question is any sentence which has an interrogative form or function. In an educational context, questions are defined as instructional queues or stimuli that convey to the participants the content elements to be learned and directions for what they are to do and how they are to do it.

So, what are the purposes of questions within the training context?

They can be used to:

- Develop interest
- Motivate the participants active involved in sessions
- Evaluate participants preparation
- Development of critical thinking skills
- Encourage inquiring attitudes
- Review previous sessions
- Summarise session content
- Nurture insights by exposing new relationships
- Assess achievement of the session goals and objectives

Training sessions which include questions prove more effective in producing achievement and gain than simple instructional, presentation based sessions.

Consider your own experience. Many of us have sat through strict, instructional training sessions or presentations disguised as training sessions. Consider your motivation, ability to focus and interest level. Think how much you actually learned and how difficult that learning process was.

Now compare this to sessions where you were engaged, where the trainer or facilitator drew you into the session using questioning and exercises. Where you were challenged and encouraged to think for yourself.

How important is it to you that the outcomes are your own conclusions irrespective of whether or not you are guided there?

Provided the environment is comfortable and safe people enjoy being challenged. Those attending training sessions enjoy being stretched and encouraged to think rather than simply listening to a presentation.

So, using questions will involve people and retain their interest. It will also have the added benefit of encouraging them to like you. Questions prove beneficial when building rapport.

Question types

In its most basic form there are two types of questions; questions can be either open or closed.

Closed questions

Closed questions can be answered "yes" or "no" or invoke a limited piece of information.

So, "Do you come here often?" "Have you been on holiday?" "Was it a nice resort?" would be examples of closed questions.

Closed questions can be used in several ways:

When confirming understanding,
"Am I right in thinking ……. ?"

When closing, "Is everyone okay with that?"
"would you like to take a break or are we okay to move on?"

The first word of the question determines whether or not the question will be open or closed. Closed questions tend to begin with did, can, would, have etc.

Open questions

An open question will elicit a great deal more information. Although any question can receive a longer answer, open questions deliberately seek the increased information.

Rudyard Kipling wrote a short poem outlining the power of these questions;

> *I keep six honest serving men*
> *(they taught me all I knew);*
> *Their names are what and why and when*
> *And how and where and who*

Open questions utilise one or more of the following six words:

```
WHAT
    WHY
        WHEN
            HOW
                WHO
                    WHERE
```

Kipling referred to them as his six honest serving men and quite rightly stated that they could never be overused. They ask the respondent to think and reflect. Open questions elicit opinions and feelings.

An inaccurate perception of open questions is that they hand over control to the respondent as it is they who will subsequently be doing most of the talking. In actual fact a series of cleverly constructed questions will allow the people asking the questions to maintain control and pass only the perception of control to the respondents.

Consider the following situation; you walk into a room where two people are sat embroiled in conversation. One person appears to be doing the vast majority of the talking. Who would you assume is in control? The general assumption is that it is the person doing the talking. Actually it is the person listening. They are the one asking the questions and as such it is they who determine what is being talked about. They guide the conversations path by demonstrating active listening and employing good use of questions.

Asking open questions will again help with the rapport building process (to be discussed a little later). People love talking, they adore talking about themselves. Asking open questions elicits their thoughts and feelings. In asking open questions we are demonstrating interest in them. This makes them feel special and important and unconsciously they recognise that the person asking the questions is the one bringing about these feelings within them.

When you are having a conversation, the most interesting person is not the one doing all the talking, it is the one doing all the listening. Remember, people love talking, they adore talking about themselves. Ask questions then listen and you are allowing them to do just that. As a result, they will think you are incredibly interesting.

Why? You are demonstrating an interest in them!

In a training environment this is no different. The participants want to talk. They have thoughts and opinions which they want to share. Whilst ever we create an environment where people feel comfortable to do so, they will share these thoughts opinions and feelings and will allow themselves to be guided where necessary.

Employing these questioning techniques

Questions are employed when we want to get into deeper detail about a particular issue. There are often signals which indicate that a participant is thinking something and not saying it. What they actually say is often severely abbreviated from what is intended or what they may actually think.

Peoples thoughts are generally censored resulting in them assuming that things are already known. This often manifests itself in vague words or statements that indicate that there is more to know. Alternatively the participant may well have already come to a decision implying a judgment of some kind. Questions can be used to clarify detail. The participant may have made some brief comments on which we would like them to elaborate and expand. Use of searching questions will lead them to reveal more about this area of interest.

Using open questions will encourage them to air their views. When doing so it is possible to make it easy for them to answer by being relaxed and casual, demonstrating open body language and good eye contact, to listen without bias or prejudice.

Questioning in a training environment

Asking an individual

People learn in different ways and not everyone needs to be active in every discussion in order for them to appreciate and take on board information. In fact, forcing people who would otherwise prefer to adopt a reflective approach to "join in" can be detrimental to their learning as it increases stress levels, making them feel uncomfortable. If the right environment is created participation will be received from all present. In some cases however, it may be necessary to direct a question to a single member of the group.

The temptation may be to attract their attention by stating their name and follow this with the specific question. There is a problem with this approach. Whilst we only want this one person to answer the question, we still want everybody else to hear and reflect on it. If we say the person's name first the remainder of the group will focus more on the individual and *how* they answer the question rather than their own answer to the question.

A way to mitigate this effect is to ask the question first, then look at the individual and say their name.

"How would that be dealt with in a branch...... John?"

Asking the group

It is important to create an environment where people feel comfortable to share their thoughts and feelings. There are many strategies which may be employed to facilitate this. Be generous with praise regarding people's responses. Actively listen and don't interrupt. Review the "power of yes" section found later in this book, it's a powerful tool!

How you respond to points made will signal to others what to do next. If participant's views are criticised then few others will volunteer. If they are praised or otherwise rewarded, which can be as simple as showing interest or offering thanks, then they and others will be more motivated to respond.

Eye contact is incredibly powerful when dealing with the group. If we simply want any member of the group to answer the question, ask the question then scan the group offering the equivalent level of eye contact to each member until somebody answers. If the group are reticent to answer hang on a short while then direct eye contact to one individual. They will generally answer at this point. Once they have finished their answer it is important to "let them off the hook". Thank them for their input, take a step back and open the question back up the group.

It is important to get the group to actively participate in the session, even if doing so initially feels slightly uncomfortable. If nobody offers an immediate answer the temptation is to answer your own question. This sends a negative signal to the group and will create further issues as the session progresses.

If this tactic doesn't work and having waited a moment a further option is to now direct the question to one member of the group. This can make people feel slightly uncomfortable so it is important to consider how this is done. Use the more confident members of the group early on. Rather than simply stating their name, ask a supplementary question such as "what are your thoughts on this John?"

If you are still struggling to elicit responses it pays to be honest. Explain that the day will work far better with interaction. Tell them that you want to elicit their opinions and thoughts. That it is their day and their input will be welcomed.

Training techniques when asking or answering questions

Scanning

Continue to use eye contact. Keep looking around to see whether people are showing interest, confusion, frustration etc. and then respond accordingly.

Multiple conversations

In an open forum do not allow more than one conversation to take place. It demonstrates bad manners to the individual who is answering your question if you allow other people to talk at the same time and you will soon lose control if you allow it to continue.

Keywords

Employing keywords is a way of creating a comfortable environment and allowing participants to feel important and that their views are valued. When the participant speaks they will employ a key word or phrase. Repeat this phrase back. It emphasises that you agree and that you feel it was a good point which was well made. For greater impact, remember the word or phrase and reuse it a short while later. This will not go unnoticed by the participant and has a hugely positive effect.

Bringing a discussion to a close

To steer the group towards the end of the session, summarise the session perhaps allowing a few more inputs to allow people get things off their chest. Offer a brief time frame which will determine exactly how much more discussion you want on the topic and welcome final inputs:

"We are going to need to wrap this up in the next 10 minutes, who has any last comments?"

Words like "last" indicate that you are looking for only a few more inputs.

Always end with thanks and praise. You will then hopefully move into the next session with a positive and motivated group.

Redirecting questions

How many trainers does it take to change a light bulb?
How many trainers do you think it takes to change a light bulb?

Throughout the training session the participants will ask you a great number of questions. Remember;

80% of questions are statements in disguise.

It is surprising how often participants ask questions even though they already know the answer. Uncertainty about whether their thoughts are correct or a lack of confidence makes them reticent about making a direct statement so they pose a question instead.

In the training environment we are seeking to stimulate independent thought and both stretch and challenge the participants. As we know, the participant will invariably have an idea about the answer to their own question. If they don't, somebody else within the group will. Rather than simply answering their questions, either bounce the question directly back to the person who posed it, open it up to the group or redirect it to a specific individual.

This technique has many benefits.

Firstly, the participants need to have confidence in the trainer. Your credibility is all important. Whilst you will probably know a great deal about your subject you may not know everything. If you try to answer all the questions asked of you, it will become apparent when you reach the question which you can't answer. The participants will pick up on this and it will have a negative impact on their view of you and therefore on the session as a whole.

Secondly, if you answer every question which is posed, it may be perceived by some as "showing off" which will again have a negative impact on your credibility.

Finally, if you answer the question the participants are not been challenged. Throwing the question open to the group will stimulate discussion and directed learning.

Body language tells

We will cover body language in more detail a little later on however here are a few body language tells to be aware of.

If a trainer is asked a question to which they do not know the answer or are caught slightly off guard, they will often take one step backwards. It is a perfectly natural physiological response. If they don't take a full step, they will put one foot backwards slightly and lean back on it, often folding their arms across the body or placing one of across the body, holding the elbow of the second arm, the hand of which is extended to the chin. You may have come across the phrases "take a step back", "I was taken aback" or "look at it from a different angle". These often refer to situations where we are unsure of a particular outcome.

When you perform any of these movements the participants unconsciously pick up on the fact. Beware of the unconscious desire to take a step back. If you're entering into a discussion around a topic which is relatively unfamiliar to you take steps which will mitigate these actions. Perch on a desk or sit down. Change your physiology in some way.

Question techniques to be aware of

Double bind questions

Double bind questions are questions structured in such a way that however it is answered, the result is the same. As a result you are "damned if you do and damned if you don't".

The questioning style originated in studies of schizophrenia where sufferers of this debilitating condition become trapped between two mutually exclusive demands. As a persuasive device it is incredibly coercive in nature as it seeks to deny the person questioned free choice.

Example:

"Are you lying again?"

It is posed as a closed question so that, in this example, irrespective of how it is answered, it confirms that the individual generally lies. This type of question is often employed by participants who wish to be difficult and truculent. The best response to this form of question is to treat it as an open question and respond to the assumption rather than the close section.

"What makes you think that this might be a lie?"

So, well-structured questioning techniques is the first step, the next is listening.

Listening

"That's enough about me let's talk about you……. what do you think about me?"

Most people have come across the saying "we have two ears and one mouth; we should use them in the proportion". It is a surprise then that the art of listening is often such a poorly employed skill.

Listening provides much useful information and is a good way to increase rapport yet good listening skills are so rarely applied.

Listening can add a great deal of value for the listener. Great leaders, coaches, trainers and facilitators are also great listeners.

Building trust

People who listen are trusted more than those who monopolise conversations, who talk without paying attention to those around them, where the only opinion that matters is their own.

Trust is the way to influencing and changing minds, and listening is the key.

Credibility

If you listen to someone, and listen well, your credibility increases with them and with the other listeners around them.

You will be perceived as competent, capable and judged as working with others rather than against them.

Good leaders are good at listening and good listeners are seen as potentially good leaders.

It was said of Gladstone, a 19th century British Prime Minister, that if you had dinner with him, you came away believing that he was the most intelligent person in the country.

However, if you had dinner with Disraeli, who also became Prime Minister, you came away believing that you were the most intelligent person in the country.

Clearly, Disraeli knew how to listen better than Gladstone.

Help them speak

Sometimes the speaker is having difficulty getting their point across. Maybe they are not all that good at speaking or are seeking to explain a complex concept. It is possible to help them and yourself by offering positive encouragement.

If they lack confidence, encourage them with nods, smiles and positive noises. Show that you are interested in them.

Asking positive questions is a generally good approach, both to test your own understanding and also to demonstrate interest.

Active listening

Positive encouragement

Active listening offers positive encouragement using attentive body language and encouraging words and actually helps the other person to speak and feel good about what they are saying.

There are three stages to active listening:

- **Hearing**
- **Attention**
- **Understanding**

Rather unsurprisingly, it is important that we first hear what is being said. As we will see, this is not always as straight forward as it first appears.

Next, in order for the person to keep speaking, it is important for them to know that we are hearing what has been said, that we are paying attention.

Finally it is important to confirm that we have understood what has been said.

1. Hearing

To paraphrase Yogi Berra:

"You can hear a lot just by listening"

In its most basic form, listening is simply hearing what is being said. Unfortunately, hearing what is being said isn't always that simple.

People tend to speak at 2-3 words per second, so between 120 and 180 words per minute. The human brain, in all its complexity, can absorb information at the equivalent rate of between 900 and 1000 words per minute. So when we are listening to people, our brain is often racing ahead. In fact we have usually already made up our mind what the person is trying to say a long way in advance of them actually saying it!

The anomaly that occurs is unusual. Whilst the brain has the capacity to absorb every word that is said, we only actually hear about 1 word in every 5 spoken, about 20%. The brain appears to pick out what it considers to be the salient points and processes the information in order to quickly make a decision on what exactly is being said.

This can have a hugely negative impact on our ability to listen. During a conversation there are few things more irritating than being interrupted by the other party who begins telling us exactly what we mean.

Also, we are information gatherers by our very nature and information surrounds us. Our senses are being constantly bombarded by information in all forms which will act as a constant distraction if we allow it.

The true key to listening then is to actually hear what is being said which first entails isolating the information we are being given from all the other information which could distract us.

The human brain can apparently focus on seven things plus or minus two. So, we can focus on five very important things or nine less important things. As an average, we can focus on seven.

We are unfortunately constantly surrounded by a myriad of information. Luckily, our brain discounts a great deal of what it considers to be irrelevant information, the pile in the carpet beneath our feet, the shades and shadows of the walls that surround us, the temperature and smell of the room, the number of lights, the design of the furniture, that mark on the ceiling, the road noise from outside, a telephone ringing in another room and so on and so on.

If we are to hear what is being said, we must account for the distractions around as and set them to one side.

Distractions include:

Sensory factors

Sights

Whilst windows are obviously incredibly important as they are great sources of natural light, what can be seen can be very distracting both for the trainer and for the other participants.

Anything moving, people in particular, are distracting, even when they are not known.

Sound

A noisy room, or external noise, provides much distraction, as sound is an important element of listening. People interrupting and asking questions or even talking nearby are a particular distraction which can inhibit discussion.

Smell

The human nose is a very sensitive instrument and smells can be very evocative and so, distracting. For this reason, training in or close to a cafeteria or restaurant may not be a good idea.

If lunch is delivered during a session, even if it is set to one side, the smell and site of the food can be incredibly distracting. Rather than simply ignoring this, which will only compound the situation, do one of two things:

Firstly, you can call lunch at this point. If it is not possible to break up the session, then simply raise people's awareness of the distracting influence of the food by simply mentioning it. Let the participants know how long it will be before they have the opportunity to eat it, then move on with the session.

Temperature

It is difficult to talk comfortably, and to listen, if it is too hot or too cold.

Temperature in the training environment is always important, and whilst sometimes difficult to judge, it is an integral factor in maintaining energy levels and attention.

Physiological factors - Discomfort

If the listener is uncomfortable in any way, then their discomfort acts as a distraction and reduces their ability to talk or listen. This discomfort can be physical, brought about by poor room setup or by the furniture.

Fatigue

As people become tired, especially after a hard day's learning, irrespective of how much fun they are having, their ability to concentrate and listen will be diminished.

Simply hearing what somebody says, whilst a good start, is not enough. It is important that that person *knows* you are hearing what is being said, that you are *paying attention*.

2. Attention

Give your full attention.

When somebody is speaking, it is very important for them to know that the person with whom they are speaking is listening. Paying attention to them. Give them your full and undivided attention and do so visibly. Attend with your ears and with your whole body. Face them and maintain good eye contact.

The trick to giving your full attention is to do it from inside your head. Interest is often just a matter of attitude and if you can be truly interested then your body will happily follow your mind.

Be considerate of the other person and help them feel good about themselves. Having someone pay close attention to you and show interest is very flattering and feels good. A fundamental attitude which supports this is to value and accept all views and opinions, even if you do not agree with what they have to say or how they say it.

Encourage the other person to speak by accepting both them and their arguments. Do not offer judgements or opinions. At this point your role is to listen, to gather information, opinions and views and to make the person feel good.

As a result, it is important to manage your reactions. Consider carefully how you react to what the other person says. A listener will be easily put off by someone who demonstrates a lack of interest, who simply does not seem to understand what is being said or who offers judgments, criticisms and opinions.

Pause before you offer any comment regarding what has been said. Consider what you're about to say and the impact that it will have.

Is this the impact you want to achieve?

So the person speaking wants you to hear what is being said and demonstrate that you are hearing it. The best way to confirm that you have done both of those is to demonstrate that you also understand it.

3. Understanding

The best way to confirm that you have been listening is to demonstrate your understanding of what has been said. This is best accomplished by giving back their information in the form of a summary. This is not simply repeating what has been said, as this does not demonstrate understanding. We would look to condense the information that has been given in the form of a brief summary.

This encompasses two goals.

Firstly, it confirms we have been listening.

Secondly, it corrects the incorrect. If we summarise information and give it back to them, anything that we may actually have heard incorrectly, or misconstrued, will be corrected at this point.

The power of yes

It is important to maintain interaction with the participants. This interaction enables the trainer to confirm the understanding of the participants as the day progresses. It aids both the flow of the day and of the information. It makes the sessions more interesting for both the trainer and those participating as well as helping to maintain the participants buy-in and commitment to learning.

People rarely enjoy being told, they much prefer coming up with their own conclusions, so rather than simply telling, it is important to ask.

So, if the trainer is to maintain participant interaction, it is important that the participants feel comfortable when interacting.

Consider how you react when somebody says "No" or "you're wrong!" in response to something you have said.

When we ask a question we want someone who may not be totally comfortable with their own response to offer an answer anyway. If a response is volunteered and is subsequently criticised in any way, through our language, either verbal on non-verbal, it is important to consider how a participant may react:

> With annoyance?
> Visibly upset?
> Frustrated?

How might their subsequent behaviour change?

Aggressive?
Defensive?

None of these are good reactions and will adversely affect their future interaction.

So firstly, it is important to avoid reacting to any statement with the words "no" or "you're wrong"

Whilst the response may not always be given specifically using the words "no", or "you're wrong!", we often use language which evokes the same responses. It is just that we first convert it into "trainer speak":

Trainer Speak	Translation
"not really"	no
"not quite"	no
"it's a good answer....it's not right"	You're wrong
"let's just park that...."	You're wrong
"okay, we'll put it on the flip anyway..."	You're still wrong
"I've never heard it put that way before"	You're criminally insane!

Referring to the Arc of Distortion (to be covered a little later, in the communication section), we can consider how our message may be received.

The art is to simply respond "Yes" to all suggestions.

This can then be followed by a reason by why the answer is correct, even, if on the face of it, the answer appears contradictory to what was being requested.

The power of yes

In the participants mind there is some validity to what they have suggested. Find it and confirm it back or seek out some truth and change the answer into a positive a response.

My own experience

When I was first exposed to this concept I remember responding with pride, stating that I never disagreed with a participant. I never said "no". The trainer quite rightly pointed out that there is a big difference between "never saying no" and responding with "yes".

Your response should begin with the word "yes" then turn the response into a correct answer.

Practical Application

Good trainers and facilitators understand how to respond to any suggestion made by a group of people. They will begin by opening their response with the word "yes". They will then pick out a positive aspect of the idea and shift the entire response in line with the desired and correct outcome. This technique creates a correct response from the original suggestion. Here the person does not feel disregarded even though the idea may not originally have appeared to hold any value. They have been paced and then led into a better idea and it will appear as though they originally came up with it. A good technique to use when given an answer which differs from what was expected is to act as if the individual has spotted something at a deeper level than that of the subject originally being discussed. The idea can then be led around to the desired answer without making the individual feel uncomfortable.

Whilst this is possibly one of the more controversial aspects of training practice it is the one which constantly attracts the most positive feedback from those participants who experience it. Many participants have taken me on one side, or passed comment in front of those others attending on the positive impact of this technique. They feel valued and able to respond to any question, even if they are unsure of their response. Where they would previously have been reticent about offering a response for fear of the derision they may encounter, they feel confident to "have a go". This feedback has been received on many, many occasions. They state that the way in which they were treated inspired confidence and allowed them to feel comfortable to offer any response, no matter how silly it might originally seem in their own mind.

Praise and Recognition

Offering thanks and giving praise is so easy and costs nothing yet they are the most commonly overlooked and under-estimated methods of motivating people.

Looking someone in the eye and thanking them with sincerity it means a great deal and evokes a powerful response. When employed in the presence of others the effects are magnified.

Offering thanks is most effective when it is natural and given from the heart, when the thanks are well intentioned they will be well received.

Key words to use are those which say thanks and well done for doing a great job. They are especially effective when they recognise the individual's contribution, their abilities and effort.

People genuinely appreciate sincere thanks. They appreciate being valued as an individual even more. Take the time to seek out a participant's unique contribution, the special thing that each person has done or given and make a point of mentioning these things. Aligning the praise with specific actions carries greater meaning and enhances its motivational effect.

Repetition is the mother of all learning

Repetition is the mother of all learning

The human brain thinks at between 900 and 1000 words per minute however we only speak at between 120 to 180 words per minute.

The brain therefore requires a great deal of activity to keep it entertained and enthused. In fact, the brain is so good it has invariably made up its mind about where a conversation or sentence is going long before the sentence is completed. Have you ever found yourself in a position where you are trying to tell somebody something and halfway through they interrupt, arguing with you regarding what you're *about* to say?

The human brain has a filtration mechanism which restricts the flow of information going to it. It picks out only the information it considers to be relevant, usually as little as one in five words. As a result we only hear about 20% of what has been said to us.

Try these on a friend:

Ask them:

"How do you spell shop?"

Look at them questioningly so that they understand that you actually want them to spell it out.

Confirm it back to them, "So you spell it S – H – O – P?"

As they nod their agreement, quickly ask:

"What you do at a green light?"

The right answer is of course "go" yet you will be amazed at how many will answer "stop", look slightly confused for a moment and then correct themselves.

Basically, the human brain picks out what it considers to be relevant information it does not listen to every word spoken. The brain also works by association and as we can see, is easily misdirected. In this instance it is thinking shop and is probably visualising the word shop. Halfway through your question it has already decided what the answer will be.

Now see how they get on with this one:

Ask them:

"How do you spell silk?"

Again, look at them questioningly so that they will actually spell the word out loud.

Confirm it back to them:

"So you spell it S – I – L – K?"

Again, as they nod their agreement, quickly ask:

"What do cows drink?"

Even if they get the right answer which is of course water, ask them if they originally thought the answer was milk.

This is a good demonstration of how information can be misconstrued and misinterpreted and how this very often leads to it being misrepresented.

So, how do we overcome this issue?

Simple:

Repetition followed by **repetition** with further **repetition!**

Why is it that when people hear a song, they can invariably join in with the chorus yet find remembering the verses more difficult?

The fact is the chorus is repeated several times so they have heard it more often. It's as simple as that. Repetition really is the mother of all learning.

It is possible to go and see a film and thoroughly enjoy it yet, when you watch it for a second time, you spot something which you missed the first time around. Often the film can be watched for a third or fourth time with us still spotting something new.

The fact that we didn't catch all the information first time around doesn't mean that we didn't enjoy it or that we didn't take a great deal from it, it is simply that the human brain can't process that amount of information over that space of time and pick up every single piece of relevant information on the first attempt. Until we have processed information more than once we might not realise which bits are actually relevant.

So how can we use this information to help the process of learning?

Repetition is very important when helping people learn. Unfortunately, obvious repetition can be very frustrating.

The trick is to repeat the information as often as possible without it appearing that we are repeating the information as often as possible.

Following are tactics which can be used to repeat information in a participant friendly manner:

Tactics for repetition

- Employ different methods to get the same information across.

- Use elements of presentation as well as group or syndicate work.

- Encourage the participants to present the information back themselves.

  When this is done, use different techniques, on one occasion you might ask them to write up everything on a flip chart, on another they may be asked to present the information back using only pictures.

- Summarise the information at the end of each session; dedicate some time to review information each morning on longer courses.

- Post relevant information on the walls. Have posters prepared and laminated which you can use on different courses.

- Take photographs of any information posted on the walls and circulate around the group electronically.

- Post the participants work on the walls, stick their flip chart paper on the walls.

- Throughout the sessions, break the information down into small manageable chunks.

- Loop a PowerPoint presentation showing key phrases on each page and cycle these during breaks.

- Encourage the participants to create acronyms, limericks or poems which reinforce relevant information.

- Use stories or parables which reinforce key points.

- Design sessions so that they follow a logical flow and link each session together by reinforcing the common information.

- Issue short handouts throughout the day.

- Make these short handouts simple, with very limited information. This will make them easy to read and increase their impact. Emphasise only the key points. Make them no more than one-page and very colourful.

- Vary your delivery media throughout the day.

Giving feedback

What is feedback?

Feedback is an integral part of human communication.

Communication

Give Information

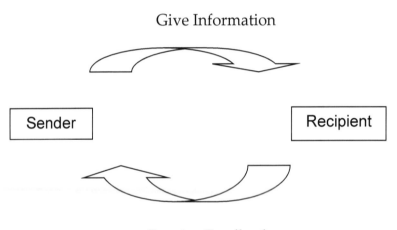

Receive Feedback

Within effective communication a message is given and information is received back regarding that message. The information received is called feedback. Someone is literally "feeding" information "back" to the provider of that information.

In normal communication this process happens seamlessly with few people even recognising or appreciating the fact that they are offering feedback.

Good communicators have honed their skills of listening to messages and then feeding back or responding in a positive and constructive way. The facets of effective communication are examined later in this book.

Feedback for development purposes

Within a training context if feedback is to be well received and acted upon, it needs to be well constructed, well intentioned and well delivered.

The art of giving constructive feedback is one of the most crucial aspects within any trainers portfolio of skills.

What is effective feedback?

Effective feedback provides a combination of positive areas which re-affirm the skills and knowledge which already in existence as well as areas in which development will enhance future performance.

Effective feedback considers the feelings of the learner. It should be motivational and encourage and aid development in a positive way.

The best way to ensure feedback is motivational is to ensure that it provides a *boost!*

Feedback should be:

- **Balanced**
- **Objective**
- **Open**
- **Specific**
- **Timely**

Balanced

Balanced refers to the need to offer information which reinforces positive behaviour as well as focusing on those aspects of the learner's performance which will benefit from development, a combination of both positive reinforcement and areas of development.

Objective

Objective feedback is that which is free of bias. Remove all subjective opinion from the feedback process. Focus on the behaviour rather than the person. State clearly what was seen and what was heard. Offer statements of fact rather than thoughts or opinions.

Open

Areas of development are thought by some to be weaknesses and considered negative. As such, many people find it difficult to offer this information to others. They feel uncomfortable describing what they consider to be negative aspects of a person's behaviour.

Being open, refers to the ability to actually give the information required of the learner. If an individual is to improve it is important that they receive feedback. This feedback will highlight a learner's strengths and areas in which they can develop. As such, it is important that this information is given.

Be open, be honest. Give both positive reinforcement and areas for development and give them freely.

Specific

Offer specific information. Feedback should be unambiguous. The learner should be left in no doubt as to exactly what is meant, which areas are good and which require development. Consider language very carefully. It is not sufficient to say that a general area was good – offer clarity as to which area is being discussed and clearly state its strengths and development areas.

Timely

The impact of feedback diminishes over time. Offering feedback on an activity which occurred some time ago will have less impact than if the feedback is offered immediately. Ensure time is available for feedback as close to the event as possible.

Working the group

One singer, One song

If you are working with a group as a whole it is important that the group works as a whole. If you want to stimulate separate conversations, demonstrate that this is acceptable by breaking the group down into smaller subsections. If not, it is important to keep all discussion within the main forum.

Multiple conversations

Occasionally, separate discussions will break out within the larger group. If you allow separate conversations to break out you will ultimately lose control.

People are generally well mannered and polite and do not talk over somebody else intentionally or out of malice. Stopping this behaviour is relatively easily done by employing the following steps:

Ground Rules

Include a section in your introduction which lays the ground rule of manners. Explain at this point that everybody has a right to speak and be heard. Everybody's view is important and so you would respectfully ask that when someone is talking everyone else should listen. We will all get the opportunity to speak. If an issue arises, simply remind them of this conversation.

Set a President

Do not allow any multiple conversations. Stop this behaviour when it first appears. Doing so will set a president that this is not acceptable and will actually make reinforcing this simpler in the long run.

Who speaks first?

If two people begin to speak at the same time, look from one to the other and simply ask who would like to speak first.

Separate conversations

If somebody within the group is already talking and a separate conversation breaks out, turn to the people who are speaking and politely ask if everything is all right. They will generally appreciate the point you're trying to make, apologise and listen to the person who had begun speaking. If the problem persists remind the group (so as to not single out anyone individual) of the earlier conversation regarding people's right to speak and be heard.

Handling third party interruptions

If one person continues to interrupt or start separate conversations, this is a situation which must be dealt with. The remaining members of the group deserve to be treated with courtesy and manners. Always deal with any situation like this in private. Call a break and immediately call this individual to one side. Do this so that it is obvious to the group that you are having this conversation. This will send a message to the group that their views are important and you will not tolerate rudeness and discourteous behaviour. This will be well received from the group. Politely explain to the individual what they are doing, and the impact it will ultimately have on the group. Allow them the opportunity to rectify the behaviour. Most people will. If they choose not to rectify the behaviour and persist in this manner, escalate the issue. Again, do this in private.

What if somebody asks a question?

If a participant asks a question or makes a comment, stop talking and stop moving. Turn to face them and give them your un-divided attention. Mirror them by matching the pace and cadence of their speech by nodding in time with its rhythmic beating.

Everybody's speech has a rhythm or tempo. Like the beat of a song or the rhythm of a poem. When we have unconscious rapport we automatically fall into this rhythm and copy it when nodding or with the "verbal" nods we use to signify agreement and encouragement.

When they have finished speaking or have asked their question, return your attention to the group as a whole.

What if someone else begins to speak at the same time?

If they are agreeing, give them a positive gesture and return your attention to the original speaker.

Again, when the speaker finishes, share your attention with the rest of the group.

It is common when one person speaks for others to begin speaking amongst themselves. If you allow a separate conversation to break out you will lose control and pass on a poor message to the group as a whole. Do not allow separate conversations.

To the person who first spoke raise your head, eye brows and hand very slightly to indicate you require a pause and excuse yourself. Refer to the separate conversation and end it using the strategies discussed above. Give your attention back to the original speaker and apologise for interrupting them.

The remaining participants will appreciate this respectful gesture as much as the "speaker". It signifies that manners are important and that they will be listened to. It also reinforces the fact that their thoughts and opinions matter and will be heard without interruption.

Working the group

Tell people what to do rather than what not to do

When offering instruction, tell people what is expected or required of them. Tell them what to do rather than focusing on what they shouldn't do. Whilst this sounds obvious, when giving instructions many people focus on the negative rather than the positive aspects of the actions involved. The human brain is like a magnet, we are drawn to that which we think about.

Many instructions that are offered cause us to think of the negative aspects of actions:

"Don't do that" or "remember not to do this".

Being told what *not to do* results in that negative action being at the forefront of our minds. We are then drawn to these negative aspects and this is reflected in our actions.

Offering positive, specific instructions will make it far easier for people to complete the actions that are required rather than focusing on not doing what isn't!

Control your fear

Be conscious of actions that will betray your nerves. Holding a piece of paper will magnify the effect of shaking hands. The tremble in your legs will increase if you stand in one position.

Accept the fact that your mouth will go dry early in a training session so have a glass of water to hand. There are many actions you can take to counter the perfectly natural effect of nerves have on your physiology, refer to section "fear of public speaking".

Dress to impress

Dress 10% better than you expect the participants to dress. Wearing comfortable loose fitting clothes will help maintain a relaxed approach.

Dealing with Difficult Participants

Ideally everybody attending a training course would do so with an upbeat and positive approach to learning. Whilst the majority do, this idea of learning still creates fear and therefore reluctance in many others. There may be many reasons why this is the case.

Possible triggers for reluctant learners:

Bad past experience

There is a strong possibility that people have attended training courses in the past that were poorly organised, poorly constructed or poorly delivered.

Bad past experience of formal learning events may mean that they view attending a training course as a punishment rather than a privilege.

Personal criticism

People can be surprisingly insecure. An invitation to attend a training course could be taken as a personal criticism. After all… "they would only ask me to go on a training course if I'm doing something wrong!"

The need for learning may suggest they're not good at what they do.

Fear of change

Organisational change outside the training environment may cause them to bring apprehension into the training environment.

Happy with the status quo

Attendance on a training programme invariably involves doing something different or doing something differently. In other words on completion of the course, the participants may be required to implement new strategies or alter those which currently exist. When people have created processes and habits which are comfortable, the requirement to adapt or innovate can be met with resistance.

Issues outside the office

Issues unrelated to work such as personal/home worries can affect an individual's desire to learn.

Lack of confidence

Not everyone relishes the opportunity to talk in public or meet new people. Training works in groups and the thought of being immersed in a group of new people can be intimidating.

Been there... bought the T-Shirt

Some people have an issue with training because they have "seen it all before....!"

Let's be honest, if they have been with the same organisation for more than five years, they probably have seen it all before (or at least think they have).

Business tends to be cyclical. Things change. Sometimes to some employees, it feels as if things change just for the sake of it. Every few years a new concept or theory is unleashed on the industry. Whether as the result of a new corporate structure, change of management team, business imperative or organisational development, the latest "shiny new object" is unveiled and cascaded throughout the company.

Whilst at a corporate level we recognise the importance of this change, at a procedural level, the change may appear formulaic and therefore unnecessary.

Whatever the reason, reluctance towards learning may manifest itself as difficult behaviours. Even the nicest, most reasonable individuals may demonstrate difficult or challenging behaviours if they are experiencing negativity brought about by these or other natural concerns.

If we are to help them learn, we must first help them overcome their reluctance to learning.

Standard tactics for dealing with reluctant learners

1. Start to position each participant at the very beginning of the course

Begin contracting the learning process right from the outset, almost as they first set foot through the door. Create the right environment and demonstrate a positive attitude from the fore.

As you open the course encourage them to consider why they are there. Ask questions and have them ask questions of themselves. Actively seek out a commitment to learning.

Firstly, do this on a Conscious Level:

What do you want to achieve as a result of being here?

How will you know you have achieved this?

What are you prepared to do to make this happen?

Aim to eliminate any excuses they may be holding inside:

How might you stop yourself achieving this?

Now, on a Subconscious Level:

In what other ways might you sabotage your own learning?

What may inhibit you achieving these goals?

We may expect to receive responses such as:

- External worries
- Fear of failure
- Afraid of feeling exposed
- Allowing lack of confidence to take over
- Being influenced by the negative attitudes of others
- Being unprepared to try new things

This reluctance to learning has originated from somewhere. It is important not to attack these individuals. Provoke thought where possible.

2. Ensure your delivery and content is as fresh as possible

Keep tuned in during your sessions.

Observe the group and look for signals. Keep your antennae working at all times.

Enhance your content

Research your topic to add further and interesting content. Review books, DVDs, CDs, the internet. Ensure you maintain access to a reputable newspaper and keep abreast of current affairs. Short video clips found online or created for the session can be incredibly powerful.

Change things

Try new exercises and demonstrate different ways of doing the same thing.

As an example – a cure for cynicism:

We are what is known as "dual hemispheric beings". Our brain is separated into two distinct hemispheres, often referred to as the right brain and the left brain. Each perform very different cognitive functions.

The left brain deals with facts, figures, concrete data in effect, proven, existing "black and white" information. Memory is stored in the left brain.

The right brain deals with theories and concepts. New information. Imagination and dreams live in the right brain.

In effect, your left brain is like your accountant whereas your right brain is your artist. They are joined by the corpus callosum which acts as their sole route of communication.

"How does this help?" you may be asking…

If you use an exercise at any point to review elements of the course, ask them do this using only pictures. Cynicism creates negativity which can manifest itself in incredibly disruptive and challenging behaviours. Cynicism lives in the left-hand-side of the brain. Drawing using creativity which is housed on the right-hand-side of the brain. We only tend to access one hemisphere at a time. As such, if you encourage your participants to be creative or draw very early on in the course you can help banish their cynicism. This can be done during the introductions for example by asking them "What's most important thing in your life?" and getting them to draw it.

It is very difficult to be cynical when being stimulated emotionally so strive to gain a deep connection on an emotional level.

Choose your turf

You have the ability to maintain control by doing things which are outside the norm. Make use of "pattern interrupters", these are anything which take people out of their normal processes or patterns of behaviour. If your attendees expect *individual* introductions early in the course, perform this activity as a *group* exercise.

Give them something they don't expect and allow them to enjoy it.

Remember the power of environment

An incredibly powerful way of influencing an individual's behaviour can be achieved through change of their environment.

If you can control the environment, you can typically predict or create a specific behaviour.

Changing environment is uniquely powerful in changing behaviour. An individual's environment stimulates an individual's behaviour and changing behaviour is most easily accomplished in a different environment, so, the environment can be changed to develop different behaviours.

The position of chairs, furniture and the individuals themselves has a marked impact on everyone present. If you want to change an individual's behaviour, first change the individual's environment.

When a person is moved from one environment to another, especially when one is unfamiliar with the new environment, the brain has to change. It enters a period of transition and typically becomes more open to reason.

Use Indirect Instruction

Use Indirect rather than direct Instruction.

It is possible to use more direct instruction, imparting knowledge or showing and explaining things when the group is more compliant.

Give specific instructions or steps when directing or attempting to influence behaviour. Simply telling someone to stop doing something is destined to failure as it actually draws the mind and attention to the one thing you want them to stop doing. Tell them what to do rather than what not to do.

Where there is more resistance to learning, it is more beneficial to employ Indirect Instruction. Encourage them to discover the information for themselves. Employ more syndicate exercises and group work. Control the inputs to affect the output. Try to use external information, information which is not related to the core work context, then link this back to an organisational context to create relevance.

When reluctant learners become destructive participants

Every individual who attends your course has the right to feel safe and comfortable and to enjoy every aspect of this learning experience. No single participant should be allowed to impinge on this right, so destructive or inappropriate behaviour must be dealt with.

Most trainers or facilitators could provide a long list of inappropriate and destructive behaviours which they would anticipate been displayed by the most difficult delegates. Those who:

- Constantly disagree
- Constantly asks questions
- Are reluctant to join in
- Are continually talking
- Fall asleep
- Mobile phone goes off
- Won't do role-play
- Won't do exercises
- Constantly interrupt
- Always answers every question
- Tapping a pen on the desk
- Is late or is always late back from breaks
- Makes use of inappropriate humour
- Walk out

It is important to first appreciate where we will find most, if not all of these "difficult participants". Frankly, as discussed previously, they reside in our fears. I remember attending my first "Train the trainer" course many, many years ago. It was a one-week residential training course run by a very reputable Training Company in a leafy suburb of London and was, for the most part, very good.

I was fresh into the formal role of a Training Consultant, having only previously run ad-hoc training sessions as part of an Account Management position and was eager to take on the world.

During my interviews for the position of Training Consultant someone had commented that I was rather young to be training experienced Sales people and Managers. This had stuck and played on my mind. As a result, I expected this to be an issue with those attending my courses (and paying for the privilege). With this in mind, when I was asked for my "Personal Objectives" I wanted to deal with difficult participants (this one in particular although I was too embarrassed to admit it). True to form the facilitator drew many scenarios from those attending the course and we gradually formulated strategies to deal with each one.

There is an old adage which states:

> ## *What you fear you create!*

Well I now had many more difficult participants to fear!

Yes, I could handle each one. Of course I could handle each one. In fact, there was no situation I couldn't handle. I spent many hours practising.

However, what you fear, you create. The more "difficult delegates" we look for, the more we may find. Yes, there are some seriously difficult delegates; I just wonder if we don't create a few of them ourselves!

The fact is that the vast majority of people attending training courses are very nice people. They are reasonable, pleasant individuals. Where I was expecting one or two difficulties a course, in reality you will probably only come across one or two a month or even a year.

Now, don't get me wrong. There will be issues on every course we run. There always are. It's just that these are generally the pleasant, nice individuals with issues and concerns that manifest themselves in challenging behaviours. These can be handled by employing some very simple tactics so they will barely be noticed.

These tactics are easy to employ and will eventually be done automatically, if they are not already.

Where to deal with inappropriate behaviour

Typical issues which arise with course attendees can be divided into two distinct types:

- Those that can and should be handled during the session.

- Those that most definitively should be handled in private.

Whilst many participants can and will be handled during the session, certain issues require privacy in order for them to be handled correctly. Most issues occur innocently enough; some people simply can't be quiet, others may ask many questions or answer everyone that you ask. There are those who may comment on every point raised or start separate conversations. There are also those who are reticent about joining in or working in groups. Generally though, these issues raise themselves by accident rather than due to a malicious desire to spoil your session. As such they can easily be handled.

Handle in class

Everyone has both rights and responsibilities.

Each participant has responsibilities to both the session and to the trainer and in return, every participant has the right to be treated with respect and dignity.

Participants have a subconscious need for situations to be handled. People feel uncomfortable in situations of conflict and when unacceptable behaviour is being displayed. The way in which difficult situations are handled in class will impact on the credibility and reputation of the trainer.

The best way to handle any situation is to first instigate actions early on which will reduce the chance of such behaviour occurring or at least mitigate its impact. These strategies are discussed a little later throughout this book.

When situations are to be handled in class, they must be done in a way which preserves the dignity of the individual whilst not allowing them to affect the rights of the group.

If the behaviour is genuinely accidental, due to over-exuberance or poor manners, this may be handled in class with positive results. Maintain good body language and state what is and is not acceptable. If the behaviour conflicts with ground rules established at the courses inception simply state this also.

Allow people the opportunity to rectify their behaviour.

Disruptive Participants

There are however more difficult participants. These appear to spoil sessions with a mischievous intent. They may be openly aggressive or rely on passive/aggressive behaviours. Those displaying these passive/aggressive behaviours will often display some of the same traits as described previously; they just do it on purpose, driven by a desire to disrupt the training session.

If openly aggressive they will challenge every point raised, arguing with the trainer and the other participants. They will display negative body language and undisguised disdain.

They are an unusual phenomenon. They appear thick skinned and will irritate and annoy the other members of the group. Handling them correctly will enhance your credibility and actually aid the success of the course.

If handled incorrectly

The anomaly is what happens if they are not handled correctly.

When the individual elicits this negative behaviour the other members of the group will actively demonstrate their frustration. They may roll their eyes and withdraw slightly. They want this behaviour to end.

An unusual and frustrating situation can occur if this individual is handled incorrectly. They may actually be viewed by other members of the group as a victim! As such, some of the group may even begin to support them.

Openly challenging or belittling this individual during the session, may be viewed by the other participants as aggressive. All of a sudden this difficult, disruptive participant has been transformed from an irritation to a victim and if they really are maliciously trying to have a detrimental effect on the session, the trainer has played right into their hands.

Handle in private

Praise in public – punish in private!

Any situation which escalates must be handled in private. Begin by trying to rectify the situation in the open forum as previously discussed. If, however you have tried these tactics and have received a bad reaction it is important to handle this in private however in a way that allows all the other participants to appreciate this situation is being handled. The remaining members of the group deserve to be treated with courtesy and manners and they will draw strength in the knowledge that you are protecting their right to enjoy this learning experience.

Call a break and immediately call the challenging participant to one side. Do this so that it is obvious to the group that you are handling the situation. This will send a positive message to the group. They will realise that their rights are the protected and that certain behaviour will be viewed as unacceptable.

This action will be well received by the group.

Politely explain to the individual why you have drawn them to one side, what it is that they are doing which is unacceptable, and the impact it will ultimately have on the group. Allow them the opportunity to rectify the behaviour. Most people will. If they choose not to rectify the behaviour and persist in this manner, escalate the issue. Again, do this in private.

If their behaviour does not change you must be more forceful with your request. Explain that ultimately one of two things will change; their attitude or their environment. They will either change the way they are behaving or they will leave the course.

Ultimately you have the right and in fact the responsibility, to ask anybody eliciting such behaviour to leave the course. Every other member of this group has the right to enjoy this learning experience and no one member has the right to take that away.

If ultimately it means them leaving the group, that is their choice.

Strategies for dealing with challenging participants

Following are some strategies which can be employed if some general challenging behaviour is displayed.

Initially, these will be handled subtly during the session, if the behaviour persists then deal with this outside the session. In short order you will find that these tactics will be employed automatically, as part of second nature.

Head them off at the pass!

Firstly, many of the typically challenging behaviours can be mitigated or even eliminated before they are even demonstrated.

Establish rules or guidelines for the training course very early on.

It is possible to simply tell the group which behaviours will or will not be accepted. This is typically headed "ground rules" or "housekeeping" and lists the behaviours you would expect to be displayed during the course of the day. They can be interwoven within the general training housekeeping, so whilst explaining the important aspects of the facilities such as exits, washrooms and fire precautions, such things as mobile phones, language and other issues can also be highlighted.

Another way of accomplishing this which actually often carries more weight and as such is easier to enforce, is to encourage the group to come up with their own ideas as to what will and will not be tolerated by themselves throughout the course.

Through guided discussion and exercises have the participants establish a "learning contract" which illustrates guidelines for behaviours which will and will not be accepted. If the ground rules for the day are established in this way, the participants themselves will invariably insist that they are maintained.

Areas of inclusion to be encouraged are:

- Punctuality
- Behaviours
- What is acceptable
- What is not acceptable
- Language
- Mobile phones
- Any other relevant issues

If anybody now challenges these behaviours, refer them back to the contract they drew up themselves at the outset of the course.

Participants are very much like children in the respect that they enjoy boundaries.

There is generally a sense of relief and visible relaxation as ground rules or housekeeping are established. People often feel more comfortable when they understand what is and is not accepted, what will and will not be tolerated by themselves and by other members of the group.

This is a really important exercise and will have a very positive impact on the course as a whole.

Dealing with challenging behaviours

If challenging behaviours are still demonstrated there are some simple tactics which can be employed:

A participant constantly disagrees

When new information is being introduced there will be differences of opinion.

It would be unrealistic to expect people to accept change without first processing the information, and some process information externally. In raising objections they are actually thinking out loud so expect people to initially disagree with some of the information imparted.

Provided the discourse is civil, disagreement evokes discussion and discussion allows the opportunity to inspire change.

Strategies:

Allow them to share their opinion and point of view.

Use exercises and syndicate work where they can be influenced by the views of others.

Employ exercises with a more artistic feel. It is difficult to be negative and cynical when we are accessing the right-hand side of our brain.

A participant constantly asks questions

80% of questions are statements in disguise.

Often, questions are asked which are actually statements in disguise. A participant will have a thought in their head and rather than articulate it as such, will ask it in the form of question. So, rather than saying:

"What I think it is…" they will invariably ask:

"So what would happen if…"

Allow them the opportunity of formalising this thought within their own mind by reflecting the question back to them:

"What do you think would happen if…"

If they state that they do not know or are or unwilling to answer, throw it out to the group and elicit opinions from them.

This tactic has many benefits.

Firstly, by reflecting the question back to the participant you are allowing them to actually think out loud and effectively reinforce their own thoughts and beliefs.

You will also stimulate discussion and illicit the thoughts and opinions of other members of the group.

If questions are asked with the specific intent of disrupting the session, this will require a different tactic.

It will be evident from the type of questions which are asked whether or not this is done with malicious intent. If it is evident that the participant is being difficult, challenging you with awkward questions in order to disrupt the session, it is important to deal with this outside of the session. Call a break and have the conversation.

A participant is reluctant to join in

If we consider learning styles, not everybody is an activist by nature. Some people are more inclined to sit back slightly and observe others rather than rushing to the fore and being the first to join in.

If this is the reason for their reluctance, then use encouragement and create a safe environment in which they can explore the performance, rather than observation of activities.

Ask easy questions and gesture with body language to encourage them to answer, being sure to praise their response.

Another way to create an active role is to ask these individuals to adopt the role of an observer within a specific exercise. On completion, have them present back their findings. Offer encouragement and praise and allow them to feel good about participating within the activity.

You will see increased participation if this behaviour is reinforced

A participant is continually talking or constantly interrupts

Refer back to the section "Working the group", *One singer, One song* and *multiple conversations*

Also, wait until they draw breathe, thank them for their input and move on or ask for the groups comments.

Falling asleep

It is doubtful that the trainer will ever encounter somebody who arrives with a duvet, pillows and a specific intention to fall asleep. The fact is, concentrating for any length of time can be tiring. External factors such as the temperature, the time of day, their workload or personal life and occasionally the subject matter can have an influence.

Keep the participants active. Maintain interaction and employ exercises and syndicate work. When you are designing the session, create natural breaks throughout the course of the day. Be aware of the room temperature and provide water. Use your more interesting content during the "graveyard shift" experienced just after lunch.

If a participant does actually fall asleep do not ignore it. Without drawing direct attention to them and therefore embarrassing them, create a "change" in the room. Move position, make a noise, bang the flipchart maybe even call a break if appropriate, make a joke, make comment or even make a lot of noise, do not ignore it.

When they realise they have "dosed off", many people will be suitably embarrassed. It is important that you make them aware that you know they have been struggling as it helps reduce the chance of this behaviour reoccurring. Again, don't speak to them directly, simply say to the group:

"I'm looking around and I can see a couple of red faces. I know it's getting warm in here and you are all working really hard – does anyone need to stand up or walk around, get that blood pumping again?"

Look at them as you come to the end of the question, They will get the message. They rarely take you up on the offer however they also know that their card has been marked.

Now tell them how long it is roughly until the next break and confirm that it is okay to proceed.

Participant is moaning or feels "hard done to"

These participants will probably globalise their issues and use generalisations such as:

"All of my customers….", "Everyone says…." or "That always happens…."

Insist that they are specific. They may try to offload what is known as a "hot potato", that is, an issue or problem which they want to pass onto someone else. They will have specific examples. Emphasise the isolated nature of their issue. Do not allow them to pass on their problems to either you or the group.

Use the group, drawing more positive issues from the other participants. Do not allow this individual to pull the energy from the group. If required park their issue and gain commitment to move on confirming that the intention of the session is to focus on the positive aspects of the learning.

Mobile phone goes off

Head this off at the pass - Always include a section at the beginning of the day where you create the "house rules" for the sessions. Include the requirement that mobile phones should be put on silent throughout all of the sessions.

If this ground rules has been established and a phone goes off during the session, it will be met by light-hearted derision from all others present.

If the ground rule is not established and a phone goes off, wait until the phone has been turned off, apologise and state that you should have mentioned this earlier, then explain that phones should be off throughout all of the sessions.

A participant always answers every question

This could be down to eagerness or a desire to show off. Whichever it might be it is very irritating for the other participants present and therefore needs to be dealt with.

This can be handled during the session by directing questions to other members of the group.

Alternatively the trainer could employ their own body language by moving closer to the individual who is always answering and turning to the rest of the group when they next ask a question. This will have the effect of removing eye contact with that individual which is a very powerful tool.

If the behaviour continues, have a quiet word with this individual during a break. Use flattery and explain how pleased you are with their knowledge. State that you want to see if the others are taking on board the subject matter and so politely ask them to hang back a little during the next session.

If required, reward them by allowing them to support you during an exercise or discussion.

A participant is tapping their pen on the desk

We must accept that participants will occasionally display slightly irritating behaviour. It's human nature. If the behaviour forms a distraction for the other participants it is worth taking a quiet moment during a break to point this out. Everybody should be allowed the opportunity to rectify their own behaviour, and few people would want to be viewed as an irritation by their peers.

If behaviour is being displayed with disruptive intent, then this behaviour needs to be stopped.

A participant is late or is always late back from breaks

Poor punctuality or a tardy attitude to timekeeping is not acceptable. If all other participants arrive on time and one is allowed to return from breaks at will, this will have an effect on how the trainer is perceived by the group and can breed resentment between the participants.

Have a conversation with this individual and explained that this behaviour is not acceptable.

A participant makes use of inappropriate humour

Humour within a training session is good and should be encouraged. Make this point when you're establishing ground rules for the day. There is however, no excuse for inappropriate humour so also explain that this behaviour is not acceptable. It is far easier to discuss such matters before they arise and to deal with them if they arise having already had the conversation.

If somebody does use inappropriate humour do not validate this behaviour by laughing. On the first occasion, make it clear from your body language that this is unacceptable behaviour. If you laugh you validate the behaviour and it will happen again.

If inappropriate humour is used a second time comment on the fact that it is inappropriate during the next break. If required, explain to the group that this behaviour is not acceptable.

A participant walks out and leaves the course

Let them go. It is not your responsibility to keep people on the course, it is your responsibility to keep the people on the course motivated to learn.

If somebody does not want to be there you will not want them to stay on the course against their will, nor will the other participants. If they stay, there is a strong possibility that they will disrupt the course.

Closing the Course

In Chapter 4 "Designing training programmes", section 17 of Course structure emphasised the importance of the participants leaving the course on a high.

Close with a bang. Motivational videos, sayings or stories, whatever it takes, ensure the participants leave with the desire to implement their new skills and knowledge.

Whilst it is important that the participants leave on a high, it is also important that the participants leave!

Getting the participants to leave

Creating a positive learning environment, maintaining this throughout the programme and building to a hugely motivating conclusion culminates in a positive and rewarding experience for all involved.

This has a profound impact on all who attend.

Whilst this is the aim and is incredibly beneficial for all involved it often has an unusual by-product. Many will not want to leave. Like those who have lasted to the end of a great party they will want the experience to continue, squeezing out every last drop of enjoyment.

Whilst it is a big compliment and should be seen as such it also creates certain issues. This is not the end of the course for the trainer. The trainer will have worked incredibly hard across the entire course and those who have not run a training course will have no concept of just how physically and mentally draining this is. The trainer now needs to clear up and re-organise the room. Course end reports need to be completed for the attendees. General administrative tasks require completion and any issues which arose during the course now require full attention. The trainer also needs to prepare for the next training course or meeting.

It is also important to encourage the participants to leave so that this hugely positive feeling is not dulled by the anti-climax of inane conversation as well as freeing up the trainers time for administrative tasks.

The following simple strategies will encourage participants to leave at the course conclusion:

1. Before entering into the course close, first ask if there are any final questions regarding any aspect of the course.

   This is important as any questions asked after the motivating course close will dissipate its impact. It also means that there will be no reason for people to hang around at its conclusion.

2. Complete any exercises, energisers, shakers or action-planning before embarking on the course conclusion.

3. Make the final course close section fairly presentational. This will allow control of both the message and the timings.

4. Convey all the information required. Explain the process of course evaluation or post-course procedures. Issue all handouts and confirm that the participants have everything required by the course administration.

5. In other words:

Do, say and give everything you want to do, say and give!

6. Finish by:

   - Thanking the participants for their attendance, hard work and dedication.

   - Complimenting their achievements and briefly reinforcing the benefits of employing the new learning.

   - Issue your business card if not already done so.

   - Explain how much you have enjoyed the course and are looking forward to meeting them all again.

   - Have a fast-paced "feel good" track ready on the CD player/PC.

7. Finally offer a farewell with which you are comfortable, thank the participants a final time, wishing them good luck and all the best. Wait for the applause (you never know). Now stop talking, put on the "feel good" track, open the training room door and stand next to it.

This will encourage every participant to leave at the same time, maintaining the positive feeling and avoiding the awkward and difficult alternative to this course ending.

8. Shake the hand of every participant as they leave, wishing them well.

Summary

The most important aspect of any training course or programme is the manner in which it is delivered.

The most successful training activities move beyond simply imparting skills or knowledge; they help people learn. They deliver a message which stimulates a change in behaviour and does so with the approval of those participating. The course attendees offer a willing commitment to the acquisition of skills and knowledge and are motivated to apply these after the course conclusion.

Successful and effective training programmes acknowledge and accept the fact that the human brain is like a parachute in that it works best when it is open. They begin by employing Mind-accessing techniques, offering a clear rationale for accepting the skills and knowledge being discussed and motivating their use.

This ability to Mind-access begins pre-course and continues through to the course conclusion.

One of the major factors affecting the successful transfer of the material being introduced is the manner in which it is delivered. As people learn in part through experience, successful training will encourage participation, even from the more reluctant learners. The more effective training professional will have the ability to work a group, employing simple strategies which will draw the best from those present and help them draw maximum benefit from attendance on the programme.

On the surface it often appears that people fear change. Actually, they fear being *changed!* The way in which this potential change is approached, whether that change is in skills, knowledge or even attitude, may result in people becoming resistant to the change, even if ultimately it will be of benefit to them. Whilst this reaction is not rational and in truth proves counter-productive to the individual's success, more often than not it is a direct response to the way in which this change is being initiated.

Enforced change breeds resistance

When people buy-in to the need for change, the skills, knowledge or attitude involved are often no-longer viewed as change! They are considered development or as enhancements to existing skills or knowledge or simply as a new way of doing things.

The ability to bring about a mind-set which is acceptant of change, a mind-set where new skills or knowledge are embraced and ultimately applied is affected greatly by the manner in which the new skills or knowledge, the message or the *change* are being delivered, by how they are communicated.

Great course delivery and great communication skills go hand in hand.

COMMUNICATION

Communication

Rapport

Getting the Message Across

The Arc of distortion

Rapport

Verbal Communication

Non-Verbal Communication

Introduction

The way in which a training course is delivered is the most important aspect of the overall training process because it is the most visible.

Whilst all other aspects of a training course will be scrutinised and judged, it is the manner in which the course is delivered which will remain in the minds of those participating and greatly affect their desire to apply the new skills and knowledge introduced.

The meaning of a message is determined by its recipient. There is often a difference between what one person says and what another hears, between the message delivered and the message received.

As a learning and development specialist, you will be judged by how you come across when delivering your training programmes. Your ability, the way in which you come across, the way in which you utilise your skills and knowledge, your attitude and character – all of these aspects and many more will make or break your reputation within your organisation or industry.

The manner in which a message is delivered greatly affects the way in which it is received and the way in which a message is delivered is influenced by the application of some simple communication strategies.

Communication

Trust the messenger, not the message!

It is difficult to discuss communication without making reference to a study by Professor Albert Mehrabian completed in the 1960s.

Professor Mehrabian categorised human communication as being split into the three distinct areas of verbal, vocal and visual. It is probably easier to relate these two words, music and dance.

Professor Mehrabian studied each of these facets and allocated each a weighting depending on their impact on human communication. These were as follows:

Verbal	**(Words)**	**7%**
Vocal	**(Music)**	**38%**
Visual	**(Dance)**	**55%**

So, only 7% of meaning is portrayed in the words we use, 38% being portrayed in the way in which these words are spoken and 55% in the way the body is used as we say them.

So, much of our message comes from the manner in which we say words and what we do whilst we say them as well as from the words themselves.

Whilst initially surprising, these figures hold a great deal of truth. How often are we faced with politicians who are basically giving us the same message yet one appears more trustworthy (or less deceitful!) than the other? Have you ever taken a friend home and your partner or parent says "I don't know what it is about them, I just don't trust them!" yet they have said very little?

These findings apply to communication where the messages communicated by the three channels of words, tone of voice and body language are not consistent with each other. In these circumstances the observer experiences a phenomenon referred to as cognitive dissonance. Cognitive dissonance refers to a situation where the human brain is trying to assimilate two conflicting pieces of information. It is the uncomfortable feeling of frustration we experience when things simply "don't add up".

In communication terms cognitive dissonance refers to a situation where the message received via one of these three channels conflicts with one or both of the remaining two. An example in a training scenario would be if you were to pose a closed question to the group:

"Does everybody understand that?"

All members of the group with the exception of one say "yes", nod, smile and maintain a relaxed posture. The remaining participant also says "yes", the same as the others; however they shake their head rather slowly with a puzzled expression on their face whilst folding their arms.

This would be an example of cognitive dissonance. We, as observers, are trying to assimilate two conflicting pieces of information at the same time; their words (verbal communication) are saying "yes" however their body language (non-verbal communication) is saying "no".

As non-verbal communication is almost always unconscious communication we will tend to rely on the non-verbal signals. In this situation, so as not to embarrass that particular participant, we may review the information in the form of a summary towards the end of the session which reaffirms the principal points which were made. As an alternative, we could have a quiet word with that individual during a break.

This demonstrates the strength of analysing a message on all three of the communication channels verbal, vocal and visual to ensure that we fully understand what is both being said and what remains unsaid.

Communication in a training context

From the very first seconds of your meeting you are trying to break down barriers.

These barriers exist for many different reasons. The participant may have had a bad experience of training. This may be as a result of poorly identified training, their previous trainer may have employed poor training skills or they may have been made to feel uncomfortable in some way.

In these circumstances the individual will have a negative attitude towards today's training session.

Human beings are information gatherers by their very nature. We are, however, selective in the information we seek out. From the vast array of information which surrounds us we choose the information we will accept and therefore process. It is this mental process which enables people to maintain views which may be sexist, racist or perhaps ageist. They actively seek out information which confirms their view of the world.

If for example, we believe that all men are terrible drivers we will see men driving terribly everywhere. We will however choose to "ignore" any demonstration of good male driving ability.

So, for example, if someone arrives on a training course expecting the course to be poorly delivered, they will actively seek out information which confirms this view. They will look for the "chink in the armour" and whilst finding it will have a negative impact on their day, their learning and so possibly ultimately on their career, they will be pleased to have found it.

It is evident that we would find life easier if we actively sought out the positive in every situation rather than seeking out negative behaviour just because it confirms our rather skewed view of the world. As such, this behaviour is not rational. Whilst it may not be rational, it is natural. We have not always lived in such "safe" surroundings. Our ancestors spent a great deal of their time actively seeking out problems and to be fair, threats. If they did not find them and then overcome them, they simply did not survive. Appreciating the fact that this behaviour is irrational doesn't stop it manifesting itself and so it is important that we address it as early as possible so that our message will be accepted.

What we are actively seeking to build with our participants is known as rapport.

Rapport

People like people of like mind.

That is, people like other people who prove to be like them in some way.

Consider your friends for a moment. You will undoubtedly have something in common whether it is your sense of humour, beliefs, values, political affiliation, hobbies and pastimes or religion.

The effectiveness of your training will be greatly increased with your ability to create and maintain rapport. Most people, when they are getting on well, will be in a state of unconscious rapport.

So, what is it?

Rapport is the perceived affinity between two or more people.

Studies carried out on rapport show a fascinating array of mirrored behaviours that are far more subtle than body position. People in rapport tend to breathe at the same rate, blink at the same rate, adopt each other's facial expressions and use each other's language.

Unconscious rapport creates all of these things naturally and so many people believe that employing these things will therefore aid the creation of unconscious rapport.

People like people of like mind

A large part of gaining rapport is establishing common ground; it is about discovering what you have in common with the other person. Not surprisingly then the quickest and most effective way of gaining and maintaining rapport is to establish what is important to this individual and then demonstrate that it is also of importance to you. In doing so, we establish common ground.

It is incredibly difficult to find out anything about anybody by talking. The best way to find out anything is to ask questions and then listen.

Demonstrate that you are of like mind by mirroring body language and speech patterns and ask questions. Find out what is important to the participants and demonstrate genuine interest in what they say. Most people enjoy talking about themselves however don't very often get the opportunity to do so.
Your ability to build and maintain rapport quickly will prove a key benefit when training and a major differentiator between you and others in your field.

So how do we build rapport?

When meeting people for the first time there are just three things about which we can talk:

- Us
- Them
- The situation common to us both

Talking about us:

We are trying to build rapport. Our intention is to establish common ground, to find out what areas are common to both of us. It is important to remember that people love talking, especially talking about themselves and we are people too. As such, it is our innate desire to talk about ourselves. Unfortunately we cannot find out what is common to us both by talking about ourselves and so we must quell our natural desire to do just this.

Talking about them:

We can only find out what is common to us both by asking questions and allowing the other person to talk. People love talking, they adore talking about themselves. Simply allowing them to do just this will enhance rapport, our relationship building, and allows us to establish areas of common ground. Also, people are interested in people who find them interesting. We demonstrate interest by asking questions and then listening to them.

Talking about the situation:

Again, talking about the situation common to us both is a great method of building rapport provided it is the other person doing the talking.

We are basically trying to find subjects about which we can engage people in conversation however the conversation should allow the other person to talk.

Engaging people in conversation using the situation common to both of us as a catalyst works well provided it is used to engage rather than as an excuse to talk.

Getting the message across

Referring back to our study on communication we will remember that 55% of our message is based on what we look like, 38% on what we sound like so only 7% is what we actually say.

Even allowing for some variance in these numbers it is clear that the message is shaped by the messenger. It is said that communication is 10% message and 90% the messenger. Put simply, the messenger is the message.

If the messenger is believable the messenger is believed.

Simply acknowledging this fact will place any trainer ahead of the game when it comes to getting their message across.

Most people who are required to undertake training sessions, public speaking or presentations of any kind focus on the content of the presentation yet it is its delivery which is the key. Whilst content remains incredibly important it is the actions of the presenter, from a physical and vocal standpoint which will enhance the delivery and overall effectiveness of the messages delivery.

Any trainer seeks to engage and maintain the attention of a group with the aim of imparting an important message. As 93% of communication is delivery, it is important to adopt the most effective approach and simplicity is often the most effective.

When using visual aids, it is imperative to remember your relationship to both the room and the people in the room. The messenger must always remain more important than the visual aid. Too many trainers allow the visual aid to take over and often lose both themselves and the participants.

If we want people to accept our message, we must deliver it in a way which makes it easy to take on board the information.

Appreciation of some basic psychological concepts will allow us to do just this.

Where to stand?

When reading English, we do so by reading words from left-to-right.

The eye is less distracted if it sees the presenter speaking from the left. It then glances slightly right to read the visual aid. As such, when presenting information using a visual aid, always stand on the left side of the room (the left side from the audience's point of view). If you stand on the opposite side of the room (the audience's right), the natural pattern of the way we read and listen is disturbed and the effectiveness will be reduced.

From the opposite side, the eye of the viewer must navigate backward through text to find the anchor to begin reading. This extra step forms a distraction which reduces the ability of the audience to concentrate at the highest possible level.

So when setting up your training room, always have the flip chart on the right-hand side (from the audience's point of view) so that you will always be stood on its left hand side when using it. If a projector is to be used it will usually be set up in the middle of the room. Arrange the room to enable you to stand on the left-hand side of the project.

If no visuals are to be used, it doesn't matter which side of the room you present from, as long as people can see and hear you.

Choosing a side of the room is an important step in establishing your relationship with the training environment and can have a great impact on your delivery. This will be enhanced by the actual use of the visual aids.

When to sit

Ensure there is a chair available. When engaging the participants in discussion, sitting at their level is very powerful. People are more inclined to share their thoughts and feelings if they feel they are on the same level and have subconscious approval to open up. Standing up and returning to the front of the room is a good indication that we want the discussion to move on.

The Arc of distortion

The distinction between intent and impact

When communicating, we are trying to gather information. We are also trying to get our message across.

The complexities of communication often result in the true meaning of our message being misinterpreted. We perform actions wanting something to happen however something quite different happens as a result.

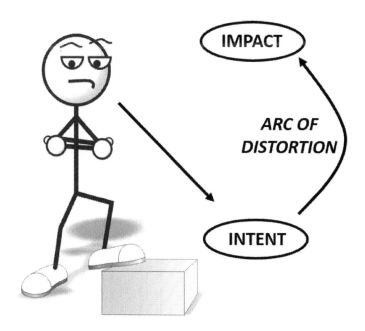

Let us consider for a moment that every human action is borne out of intent. That is, everything we do is done for some reason. So in every action, whether verbal or non-verbal, we are effectively trying to convey a message, our intent is to get something across to another party.

The issue that often arises however is that the **intent** we have does not result in the **impact** we desired or even expected. The impact does not represent our true intent.

The arc of distortion represents the difference between the message we want to send and the actual message received – the distinction between *intent* and *impact*

We can send a message expecting it to be interpreted one way however it is received in a totally different way. The message which is received being in conflict with what we actually wished to convey.

Effectively:

The meaning of a message is determined by the recipient

So, there is often a difference between the intent of an action and the actual impact that action has. It does not matter what the individual imparting the information is *trying* to get across, all that matters is what the recipient *infers* from their actions.

The difference between the two can be referred to as the "Arc of Distortion" – the distinction between intent and impact.

Mixed messages

The messenger intends to put across a certain message. They perform actions of communication, whether verbal or non-verbal with a view to putting across that specific message.

When sending the message, the messenger has the clear intent about how that message will be received.

Hopefully the message will be received in the way it was intended. The recipient however will only take their interpretation of the message as being correct.

A great example of this was given to me by a General Manager attending a course in communication skills, although I have also heard it referred by a stand-up comedian, believe it or not there is an Indian Restaurant whose motto is:

"Try our food, you'll never get better."

The restaurant is trying to get convey the message that once we have savoured the delights of their menu, we will be unable to find better fare elsewhere. The taste, quality and value offered by their cuisine is un-rivalled, they are the best in the land. Their intent is to set themselves aside from the competition and in a positive way.

Let's consider the potential impact of this statement; we could be left thinking that anyone willing to eat there will never recover. Not such a positive message.

What does this mean?

So, the Arc of Distortion exists. When it comes to getting a message across there is often a distinction between the intent of our message and its eventual impact.

So what?
What does this mean?

How can we use this to our advantage?

Let's first consider the alternative. Let us first contemplate the implications of doing nothing. There are plenty of people who do. I am sure you will know of, or will have met someone who makes statements such as:

"I know I'm a bit brash, if people don't like it that's their fault not mine."

"That's just the way I am. If they don't like it they can just take a running jump."

"If they don't like me, that's not my problem!"

Does this remind you of anyone you know?

In their own head I'm sure they feel like they are making a stand. It suggests strength of character. They are their own person and they're not changing for anyone. They are sticking to their guns. They justify they're obstinacy by viewing it as a virtue. Consider their last statement:

"If they don't like me, that's not my problem!"

Well frankly, if the "they" who is being referred to is a customer, it is very much a problem. If a customer does not like who they are dealing with does that person have a problem? Definitely, they have a big problem. Why?

People buy from people they like (and in training we are selling ourselves)

And;

People like people of like mind.

So, common sense would suggest that if we want to get on with people, rather than insisting that the entire world change to be just like us, we should offer flexibility of character and demonstrate that we are in fact, very much like them. It is the basis of rapport building. It is the basis of effective communication. Unfortunately, common sense is rarely common practise!

In life, as in training, you will often be more like others than yourself if your goal is to engage hearts and minds and be an effective communicator.

So, how do we communicate effectively?

Verbal Communication

It takes *intelligence* to understand *complexity*.
It takes <u>*true genius*</u> to simplify it.

A cursory view of the figures from the Professor Mehrabian study which demonstrated the impact on human communication (Verbal 7%, Vocal 38%, Visual, 55%) can prove misleading. On the face of it, if the words we use have only a 7% impact on human communication, this appears to suggest that words have little or no impact and so to a certain extent it doesn't matter which ones we choose.

This could not be further from the truth; try this:

If you need to close your eyes in order to do this, no problem, most people do:

Picture your house, create a mental picture of your house and remember the basic detail.

Done that?

Okay, where were you stood?

Now, let's try another one.

Again, if you need to close your eyes to do this, no problem. This time:

Picture your home, create a mental picture of your family home and remember the basic detail.

Done that?

Okay, where were you stood this time? Did anything change?

When most people are asked to picture their house, they invariably see themselves stood outside looking back at their property. This is because most people view their house as "bricks and mortar", as an investment or an asset. When asked to then consider their family home, most people move inside, often to either the kitchen or living room, this is because the word "home" is more emotive and conjures up warm images of where we live.

The words we choose, semantics, have a great impact on human communication.

Some tips regarding verbal communication:

Avoid jargon

Buzzwords and subject related terms can be useful for people who specialise in the same area as it allows them to talk in a form of "shorthand". It is often used by those who wish to signal their expertise and can, on occasion, be used in a training environment for this purpose. Most of the time however, it simply annoys other people.

Avoid complex language

There are a little over 25,000 words in the English language. Most of us however have a very limited vocabulary and only about 2000 words are used in many everyday conversations. Whilst academics and writers enjoy playing with big words, in a training environment it is often frustrating and annoying for the participants.

Those attending your training course should not have to work out what you are trying to say. Offer information in a clear, concise manner which allows it to be understood and easily processed. This does not mean "dumbing down" each training session, it simply means allowing the participants to absorb the information in a straightforward manner.

Remember names

Remembering someone's name makes them feel important, liked and happy. Use the information found in this book to help you remember everybody's name and use it as often as is appropriate.

Use positive words to challenge limiting beliefs

Phrase your words clearly and positively. Your words and the explanations you give have a great impact on the thoughts of your participants.

Participants may occasionally use gross sweeping generalisations when trying to make a contradictory or negative point. They will globalise the situation with terms like "nobody does it like that" or "none of my customers would want that". Phrases like "nobody" and "none of my" are globalised generalisations. They are incorrect and misleading and if they remain unchallenged they can create a sense of increased apprehension and apathy in the other participants. It is important to reframe these statements so as to minimise the negative impact.

Show interest and be interesting

If you become bored with a discussion it will show. Find interest in what is being said.

In line with the Arc of Distortion, adapt your material and your manner to the participants with whom you are talking. Find out what interests them and include them in the session. Your introductory meeting can often result in information that you can use during conversations or occasionally during the session provided it is not sensitive.

Actively listen. An alert face and good body posture tells the other person that you are interested. Eye contact is essential.

Use stories, jokes and anecdotes

A great way to help others understand your message is by telling a story, reading a quote or telling a joke. These stories allow the participants to relate to what you are saying or suggesting. A funny story or joke often helps people to relax. The more comfortable a person is, the more inclined they are to listen, absorb information and more importantly, remember it.

The way you deliver the story can affect the thinking, emotions and behaviour of the participants. They will imagine the experience and reproduce a response. A story can provide encouragement and inspiration. Have some interesting material and stories prepared and use them during your sessions.

Fake spontaneity!

Have stories or anecdotes prepared and use them as if on the spur of the moment. These stories will again help reinforce the point you're trying to make. The spontaneous nature of their use will also confirm your complete understanding of the subject matter in a wider context.

Vary your speech pattern

Vary the speed, tone, pitch and volume of your speech. Be aware, nervousness often causes speech rate to increase and hesitations can occur as the thoughts become disorganised. The problem may be compounded if you are asked to repeat what you have just said.

Combine humour and sincerity

Use humour and seriousness next to each other to emphasise the point you're trying to make. If you are telling a funny story, gradually increase the pace and volume as you near the end of the story. Finish the story and then reduce the speed and volume of your voice so that the more serious point is emphasised.

Use pauses. They are very effective in getting a point across and allow you to relax, take a breath and compose yourself.

If you stumble, smile and give a genuine apology, it will be well received and allow you time to think about the rest of your conversation.

Most people believe that in a crowded room shouting may be the only way to be heard; actually it is clarity of speech which helps people to understand you more effectively.

Non Verbal Communication

An individual's nonverbal communication or body language contributes immensely to the way in which they are perceived.

Demosthenes is considered to have been the greatest Athenian orator, a magnificent public speaker. When he was asked what was the most important part of oratory (public speaking) he answered:

"Action"

When asked which the second was, he replied:

"Action"

When then asked which was third he still answered:

"Action"

People tend to believe actions more than words.

In fact, much of our message comes from what is often termed our body language, or non-verbal communication.

Nonverbal communication is almost always unconscious communication and so if we raise an awareness of it, and begin to understand it, we can gain a greater insight into what people are thinking and might not be saying. It is also important to consider how our message comes across when we are communicating to our groups.

So, as we know, communication is the transfer of information from one person to another or in our case to a group of people. Most of us spend about 75 percent of our waking life communicating however, very few realise how much of our communication is expressed non-verbally.

Non-verbal communication includes facial expressions, eye contact, tone of voice, body posture, hand movements, motions, and positioning within groups.

When we communicate our messages are sent on two levels simultaneously. If the nonverbal cues and the spoken words do not match then cognitive dissonance occurs and the flow of communication is hindered. Whether correct or not, the receiver of the communication tends to base the intentions of the sender on the non- verbal cues they receive.

Modern humans are worse than their ancestors at reading body signals because we have become distracted by words.

Some points to be aware of when considering your non-verbal communication:

Physical Contact

Shaking hands, touching, holding, embracing, pushing, or patting on the back all convey messages. They reflect an element of intimacy or a feeling of (or lack of) attraction.

Touching a person with your left hand whilst shaking hands with your right hand can create a powerful result. Experiments conducted by researchers at the University of Minnesota demonstrated that skilful elbow touching can give you up to three times the chance of getting what you want.

Whilst this sounds incredible the elbow is considered a public space and is far away from intimate parts of the body and touching a stranger is not considered acceptable in most countries so this actually creates an impression.

A light, three second elbow touch creates a momentary bond between two people.

Inter-Spatial Zones

Inter spatial zones refer to an individual's appreciation and use of the space which surrounds them. As a species, man is highly territorial. We are generally only aware of it when our space is somehow violated.

Spatial relationships and territorial boundaries directly influence our daily encounters and relationships. Maintaining control over such space is a key factor in personal satisfaction.

As such, observing spatial interactions in everyday life is a key to personal awareness and effectiveness.

The study of spatial territory for the purpose of communication uses four categories of personal space:

The intimate zone
The personal zone
The social zone
The public zone

These zones radiate out from the body, the intimate zone being closest, the public zone being the widest.

The intimate zone, used for embracing or whispering is generally up to 18 inches from the body. The personal zone, for conversations among good friends and family is between 19 inches and 4 feet from the body. The social zone, for conversations among acquaintances is between 4 and 12 feet and the public zone, used for public speaking is everything which is 12 feet or more.

These are estimated figures and will vary depending on an individual's upbringing. People raised in wide-open spaces such as the countryside will tend to have wider inter-spatial zones than those raised in a busy metropolis.

Whether seated or standing it is important to stay out of the participant's intimate zone, the intimate zone being an 18 inch bubble around the body of the participant.

It is important to bare this in mind when doing exercises. People should not be made to feel uncomfortable, unless of course this is the purpose of the exercise.

You can still share a secret or touch the participant where appropriate; it simply means that when entering into their personal space, you do so strategically, knowingly and with a specific intention.

Similarly, if you leave what is known as the "casual-personal" zone, the area between 19 inches and 4 feet, you will also stand the risk of losing the participants focus. When training, ensure you keep moving to within 4 feet to maintain focus and attention.

As a relationship builds, we can gain access to inter spatial zones without causing discomfort or frustration so we could place our hand on the shoulder of a very close friend whereas if we did this with a stranger, they would probably become tense and may even withdraw.

Positioning

People have several choices regarding where they stand or sit in reference to the person with whom they are communicating.

When people are cooperating they generally prefer to stand or sit side-by-side, while those in competition frequently face one another.

We are also what are known as dual hemispheric beings, that is, our brain is quite literally split into two halves. We have a left brain and a right brain. Studies show that the left brain deals with factual, concrete, specific and proven data where the right brain deals in theories, concepts and new information.

When we are training, new information tends to go in through the right brain, is processed, and if believed, is then stored in the left brain as fact.

Take advantage of how the human brain works and where possible, keep the participants on the right hand side. This allows both parties easier access to their left-brain. This can be done when shaking hands, sitting and communicating.

Leave a chair free on the right-hand side of the group (as you look at them), slightly separated from the group. When entering into discussion with the group, sit in that chair. This will have two advantages:

Firstly, people feel more comfortable in discussions with others who are at the same level. Sitting down lets the group know on an unconscious level that their views and opinions are welcome. Open hand gestures and eye contact will still allow you to maintain control.

When you want to signify the end of this discussion period simply stand up. Where possible, as a mark of respect, wait until there is a break in the conversation. Return to the centre of the training arena.

Secondly, it places you at the far left of the group which keep the participants on the right hand side.

Body Posture

Body posture has a dramatic effect within non-verbal communication. Thought processes such as boredom, disinterest, aggression, confidence or anxiety are often overtly represented by somebody's body posture. Observing the body posture of the individuals within the group will allow you to "read" the group, giving you a feel for the success of the session.

Hand gestures

One of the most frequently observed yet least understood non-verbal cues are hand movements, especially hand to face gestures. Most people use hand movements regularly when talking. While many gestures such as a clenched fist or open palm have universal meanings, most of the others are individually learned and idiosyncratic.

Hand movements often help a description. Avoid movements that could cause a distraction. They are often unconscious so ask someone you trust to give you feedback after an active session.

Avoid pointing at all times. Pointing is perceived as aggressive and is a poor demonstration of non-verbal communication. Use open-hand gestures as an alternative.

Facial Expressions

Eye Contact

A major feature of social communication is eye contact. It can convey emotion, signal when to talk or finish, or aversion. The frequency of contact may suggest either interest or boredom.

From a training point of view eye contact is incredibly important however when people are nervous, it is invariably the first thing to go. There are many different techniques which can be employed to maintain eye contact with everybody in the room. Whilst initially employing these techniques may prove a challenge which requires conscious thought, very soon the application of eye contact to a group becomes second nature and is activated on an unconscious level.

Where should I look?

The first question is where to look. Whilst this sounds obvious "look in their eyes" this is actually not possible. At relatively short distances it is not possible to look at both eyes at the same time. One popular theory is to look directly between the eyes at the top of the bridge of the nose.

Some studies have demonstrated that increased rapport is gained by looking directly into one of the eyes.

So which one?

Depth perception is calculated as a result of our binocular vision. The brain gets two slightly different pictures, one from each eye and the convergence of the two eyes helps calculate distance. Once we extend beyond objects which are incredibly close, our left eye looks directly towards an object and the convergence of the right eye increases, in order to gain focus. The degree to which the right eye turns allows the brain to calculate how far away the object or person is.

It is an individual's left eye which is looking directly at us and studies have shown that, on an unconscious level, we prefer people to look directly to our left eye when maintaining eye contact.

Maintaining group eye contact:

The "lighthouse" technique is initially very popular. As most training sessions seat people in an arc or horseshoe, eye contact can be maintained by literary start with the person on the left and then moving around the group to the right and back again, scanning like a lighthouse.

This can become quite tedious for the participants and is a very obvious technique. The trick is to vary the scanning, missing out some people on the way round and including them on the way back. Practice will result in unconscious competence.

Control by Eye Contact

Eye contact is an incredibly powerful tool which can also be used as a form of control if required. If a participant is proving challenging for whatever reason, eye contact is a subtle way of applying control of the situation.

If a participant is interjecting a little too much, proving difficult or they have made inappropriate remarks they are automatically given more eye contact. Being aware of this and eliminating their eye contact sends a powerful sub-conscious message. After a short time period, welcome them back with a small amount of eye contact and judge their reaction.

Increased eye contact will encourage a quiet participant to join discussions.

Smile

Science has proved that the more individuals smile the more positive reactions they will receive from others. The remarkable thing about a smile is that when you give it to someone, it causes them to reciprocate by returning a smile, even if you are both using fake smiles.

Professor Ruth Campbell of University College London believes there is a "mirroring neuron" in the brain triggering the part responsible for the recognition of faces and expressions and causing it to create an instant mirroring reaction.

Basically, we automatically copy the facial expressions we receive. This is why regular smiling is important to have as part of our body language repertoire, even if we don't feel like it. Smiling directly influences other people's behaviour and attitudes and influences how they respond to us.

Humour sells

The marketing industry discovered this a long time ago. A high proportion of adverts whether they be on billboards, radio or television employ humour to engage their target audience and make their message appear more attractive.

As with smiling, when laughter is incorporated as a permanent part of who we are it attracts friends, improves our health and may extend life. When we laugh, every organ in the body is affected in a positive way. Research demonstrates that those who laugh or smile even when they don't feel especially happy stimulate the "happy" part of the brains left hemisphere.

Maintaining a positive happy approach will make us more attractive and gain better responses from the participants. By the way, the proof of the pudding is in the eating so try attending a training session or presentation run by somebody who doesn't smile and doesn't employ humour and see how much you take from it.

You never get a second chance to make a first impression!

It is important to appreciate that we have less than 10 seconds and realistically closer to 4 in which to make a good first impression on those with whom we come into contact. There is a wealth of well researched material clearly indicating that an individual will be judged both professionally and personally in the first few seconds when meeting someone for the first time.

This is a very superficial reaction and there is nothing fair or reasonable about the mental processes involved. It is an instant evaluation and to overcome these initial, instant impressions takes an enormous amount of effort. If used to our advantage, this can be a hugely positive attribute as, if our first impression is good, our training sessions will run a great deal easier.

So, how can we improve our chances of creating a good first impression?

- Be confident in your own abilities and demonstrate it.

- Dress about 10% better than your expect your participants to be addressed. This does not entail overdressing. If the participants receive a request from you asking them to dress casually, attending in business dress will have a very negative impact. It will probably be viewed as trying to gain the upper hand, creating an "us and them" mentality.

- People like people of like mind and feel most comfortable in the company of others who are very much like them. Emulate or at least be aware of the beliefs or values of your participants.

- Actively mirror. Pace and replicate body language and speech patterns.

- Show sincere interest in the participant's interest, pursuits, organisation and business.

- Remember, if you are nervous about this meeting then the participants will be as well. Utilise the operation of the brain and keep the participant on your right where possible when shaking hands, sitting and communicating.

- Whilst it is good training practice to avoid jargon, be familiar with the terminology of the participant's organisation or business. Research demonstrates that employing the language common to their business identifies you as an insider and enhances rapport.

- Greet everybody individually when they first enter the room. Use their name as often as appropriate.

- Create a warm and welcoming environment. You will be judged by it.

- Have each participants name up on the screen when they first arrive offering them a welcome message. Have the names either static, or in a revolving presentation.

- Smile.

Summary

The communication of training material, that is, the training course delivery is the most important aspect of the overall training process. This is due in part because it is the most visible and also because it is the aspect which will remain in the minds of those participating and greatly affect their desire to apply the new skills and knowledge introduced.

When it comes to the delivery of information, of communication, the meaning of a message is determined by its recipient.

All too often there is a difference between what one person says and what another hears, between the message delivered and the message received.

The way in which a message is delivered greatly affects the way in which it is received.

The ability to create and maintain rapport, to build and maintain relationships and the application of simple yet effective communication techniques will narrow the Arc of Distortion and greatly enhance the power of the message delivered.

Many people believe that "knowledge is Power", actually, the application of knowledge is far more powerful. How often do we see people with a wide array of skills and knowledge fail to convey their insights to others? Simply having an understanding of skills and knowledge, of processes and procedures, or of information is not enough. The key to effective training is the ability to share this with others. To stimulate, encourage and facilitate learning, to aid an individual's personal development and ultimately their success.

Effective communication techniques can make learning easier. They break down barriers and encourage an openness and receptiveness to new ideas and concepts. They facilitate the acquisition of new skills and knowledge and then motivate their application.

The application of effective communication techniques contributes greatly to the process of effective training.

Whilst the delivery of training material, the communication of the training message is often considered the most important aspect within a training process, it is not completed in isolation. In order to ensure that the training process is effective, that it achieves the outcomes intended, doing what it set out to do, it is important that it is evaluated.

EVALUATING TRAINING PROGRAMS

Level 1 Evaluation

Level 2 Evaluation

Level 3 Evaluation

Level 4 Evaluation

Introduction

Having identified a training or development need, designed and then subsequently delivered the training activity, the final stage of this cyclical process is to consider its effectiveness and complete an evaluation of the training undertaken.

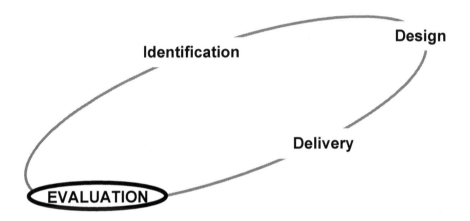

The aim of a training programme is not simply to deliver the training, creating an environment which facilitates the transfer of skills and knowledge. Training activities should be undertaken with specific objectives and outcomes in mind. Training is one of the vehicles available to an individual or organisation designed to help take them from where they are to where they want to be. In order to aid its effectiveness, it requires evaluation.

Training evaluation is designed to ensure that the original needs have been satisfied, to determine the effectiveness and efficiency of the training process.

It aims to determine the following:

- Has the training accomplished what it set out to achieve?

- Does this help the individual or organisation achieve their individual and corporate objectives? Does it help them move closer to where they wish to go?

Evaluation

Before we move into a description of evaluation methods, let's first define some key words which often arise in discussions of this topic.

Evaluation

Evaluation deals with the assessment or analysis of the overall benefits of training and development.

Assessment

The assessment of learning focuses on measuring the learners' achievements and forms part of the wider process of the evaluation of training and development. Learning objectives can specify changes in skills, knowledge and attitude. Assessment methods can focus on any one of these aspects to determine whether the learning objectives have been met.

Formative and Summative Assessment

Formative assessment

Formative assessment focuses on the actual process of training or performance improvement and is designed to enable the learner to learn or develop in the light feedback.

Summative Assessment

Here the focus is on the final product or outcome of the process and is the measurement of a learner's performance to see whether they have achieved the objectives of the programme.

The distinction between assessment and evaluation

Assessment is conducted on the individuals who have participated in the learning experience, evaluation is of the learning experience itself.

In real terms we assess the learner and evaluate the learning. We assess the trainee and evaluate the training.

Quantitative and qualitative approaches

Quantitative

With a quantitative approach to assessment we are attempting to measure performance and attach a numerical value to the performance, an example would be a score out of 10 or out of 100.

Qualitative

Quality assessment methods are not intended to be as objective. They should however be carried out in such a way as to be reliable and valid. Methods here may include observation, questioning or discussion with the participant.

Reliability

A reliable assessment is one which produces the same result irrespective of who carried it out or how many times it is completed.

Validity

Validity refers to whether or not an assessment actually measures what it claims to measure i.e. has the training done what it set out to do, has the training completed what it stated it would complete?

Training evaluation

Our training is constantly being both assessed and evaluated. Every second we spend "on our feet" is being judged by those in attendance.

Evaluation of training events can be formalised by employing the processes and strategies that follow.

It is important to first consider the participants unsolicited opinion.

People will remember the course, and us, long after the course has concluded. Our training ability and relationship building skills will help to control how well and for how long it is remembered. Our aim should be to ensure every single course we run leaves a hugely positive impact on those who attend.

The thoughts and feelings our training engenders within its participants will far outlast the course itself. It is these that create and maintain our credibility and ultimately our reputation.

If we are employed as an internal training consultant this reputation will affect our relationships company wide. If we are independent consultants, this will have a direct impact on our ability to create more work.

Formal Evaluation

Many theories in the area of evaluation stem from the work of Kirkpatrick (1967). Kirkpatrick identified four levels of evaluation:

Level 1 – The Reaction Level

Level 2 – The Immediate Level

Level 3 – The Intermediate Level

Level 4 – The Ultimate Level

In Brief:

Reaction Level: How was the training received by the participants?
What are the views of those participating?

Immediate Level: Has the course delivered what it stated it would deliver?
Can those participating do what the course stated they would be able to do?

Intermediate Level: Is the learning being applied in the workplace?

Ultimate Level: What affect has this had on the organisation?
How has the business benefited?

Each of these will be covered in turn however it is important to recognise that evaluation at all levels must be undertaken if we are to form a full picture of training effectiveness. The most important level, and therefore our focus, may differ according to circumstances and the needs of the different stakeholders. The trainer, for example will probably be more interested in how well they are being perceived within their sessions where as a Finance Director may be more concerned about the cost effectiveness of the training programs employed.

Level 1 Evaluation

The reaction level

The reaction level is evaluation generally completed during, or at the end of the training process.

This form of evaluation seeks the views of just one stakeholder, the learners themselves. It aims to establish their views of the learning event and generally does so by employing a short questionnaire completed at the end of the training session or course, or very soon afterwards.

The timing of its completion means that these are often referred to as "happy sheets", or "smile sheets" due to the fact that the learner is caught at the course conclusion where they are hopefully experiencing a natural high and feeling very motivated.

As a result, this has drawn criticism of reaction level evaluation. The criticism is brought about by worries that participants are merely reacting to the quality of the trainer's performance and ability to maintain interest or tell jokes.

There are also doubts about the ability of learners to evaluate training in its wider context.

Realistically, these questionnaires are particularly relevant when assessing the adequacy of facilities and the overall organisation of the learning event. It is often argued that these cannot provide any indicator of subsequent job performance or the transfer of learning into the work environment.

One method of increasing the effectiveness of this level of evaluation is to post forms to the participant soon after the course conclusion with a request that they complete and return the form.

The advantage of this process is to remove the pressure of completing the form in full view of the trainer and knowing that the trainer will have the opportunity to read any comments.

The disadvantage is the possibility that they may not be completed and returned or that the form may arrive when the participant is busy or distracted and so will not be a true reflection of the course.

Level 2 Evaluation

The immediate level

Immediate level evaluation attempts to directly measure the extent to which the course objectives regarding the acquisition of skills, knowledge or attitude have been achieved.

The learner is tested in some way to determine whether or not the skills or knowledge described in the course objectives have been transferred to the learners. This validation is used to confirm that the course has achieved what it set out to achieve.

Testing of the learner in effect validates the learning and therefore helps evaluation of the learning experience as a whole.

This level of evaluation can be completed on an ongoing basis throughout the course, for example by a series of structured role-plays, exam, tests and exercises, or at the course conclusion.

Level 3 Evaluation

The intermediate level

The intermediate level evaluation considers how effective the learning has been transferred back into the work environment and the overall impact of the training on job performance. It is, in effect, measuring the extent to which the new learning is subsequently being applied.

Evaluation at this level is much less common than at levels one or two, often because this form of evaluation is hard to complete and because all too often, other factors will have a bearing on whether or not the learning is applied.

> **Example:**
>
> A training course is completed regarding the sale of a new "add-on" product. If the sale of these products is not then measured, does not form part of the job role or the salespeople are not paid to sell them, they probably will not be sold.
>
> As a result, this learning may well not be applied as the individuals are not subsequently motivated to sell the new product on their return to the workplace.
>
> The learning event may have fulfilled all of its objectives however would still be judged as a failure due to the learning not been applied.

In order to complete Intermediate evaluation, several methods may be employed including observation, interviews, questionnaires or diaries.

Level 4 Evaluation

The ultimate level

The ultimate level evaluation attempts to assess the impact of training on departmental or organisational performance. The best indicators for this level of evaluation vary enormously depending upon what are deemed to be key performance criteria.

They typically include:

- Sales performance

- Customer complaints

- Returned items

- Turnover

- Productivity

- Accidents

- Absenteeism

- Staff turnover

Evaluation at the ultimate level is considered the most difficult to employ and the most problematical to use to determine the precise impact of training on overall performance.

There are many factors other than training which could ultimately affect results and therefore the evaluation. An increase in sales could be brought about by the demise of a competitor product or a change to the sales teams pay plan. In some situations there may be no clear and simple measures to employ, or data to be collected, which allows for effective evaluation to take place.

Summary

Evaluation is an integral part of the overall training cycle. There is no "one size fits all" approach to the evaluation of training activities and programmes. The aims of training evaluation will vary depending on the level at which it is completed.

Level 1 or Reaction Level evaluation elicits the views and opinions of the learners in reference to the training they have undertaken.

Level 2 seeks Immediate Evaluation either during or towards the end of the course with a view to confirming that the activities have achieved the specific training objectives. It aims to determine how close the programme and activities have come to achieving its own original goals.

Level 3 refers to Intermediate Level Evaluation which moves beyond the parameters of the training itself. It seeks to confirm whether or not the learning is subsequently being transferred by the participants on return to the business.

Ultimate Level Evaluation, level 4 seeks to assess the return on training investment and determine what effect the training has had on departmental or organisational performance.

TRAINING MEDIA

Using Visual Aids

PowerPoint

Handouts

Introduction

The manner in which information is introduced will greatly affect its impact.

A rich mix of appropriate delivery media will enhance the overall learning experience.

This of course stimulates the questions:

> What is meant by a rich mix?
> Which delivery media is appropriate and under what circumstances?

The success of any training will be dependent on many issues, not least, the Trainers ability to engage and maintain the attention of a group with the aim of sharing information or imparting an important message. With reference to the studies on human communication previously discussed, as 93% of communication is derived from the manner in which it is delivered, it is important to adopt the most effective approach and appropriate delivery media.

Using visual aids

It was Confucius who first remarked:

> **I hear : I forget**
>
> **I see : I remember**
>
> **I do : I understand**

Baden Powell very famously employed this strategy when he established the Scout movement.

We use our five senses to process information and as human beings we tend to derive a message or meaning from the information we collate.

Simply stating information can become very boring. The human brain requires a great deal more stimulation than simply hearing words and as we can see, if all we do is hear we tend to forget. Employing visual aids create a multi-sensory experience and enhances the training session.

Choosing the right visual aid

There is no one visual aid which will adequately complement all training sessions. In fact, it is said that the human brain can focus on one thing in one place for one minute before attention strays so a mix of visual aids will prove more effective.

Different visual aids will complement different areas of training sessions and the delivery of different forms of information.

For example, a flip chart is non-contrived, the information is free-flowing and so it is great for brainstorming and "blasting up" information drawn from the group. It is very de-motivating for participants to answer a question posed by the trainer, giving a long list of options, if the trainer then puts up a list of what they considered to be the correct answers on PowerPoint it is the equivalent of telling the participants that what they came up with was actually incorrect.

PowerPoint is excellent for supporting a specific message, showing pictures or images and for running video.

Again, referring back to Confucius, the ability to do something helps confirm understanding and reinforces the message being delivered. Handouts or props can be distributed and used in practical exercises.

PowerPoint

Whilst there are numerous computer based presentations available, PowerPoint remains a great medium for reinforcing information delivered during a training session. Some very simple points will greatly enhance the use of PowerPoint as a training aid.

Note: Remember to stand to the left of the screen (from the groups point of view)

Less is more

The PowerPoint presentation should complement the training session. As such each side should only contain a brief number of bullet points reinforcing the message being put across.

Many trainers fall into the trap of having too much information presented over too many sides. Unfortunately, the message which is often inferred by the participants is either:

1. The trainer has little confidence in their ability to get the information across. The trainer thinks the participants will believe the computer and not them.

2. The trainer is lazy, they couldn't be bothered to remember all the information or use a mix of delivery methods.

Neither of these conclusions can be perceived as being good and detract from the actual message.

Limit the number of slides and the amount of information per slide.

Always face the group

Many trainers succumb to the temptation to turn and face the screen, some even read from it. The bullet points are not prompts for the trainer; they are there to reinforce the information being imparted.

If the presentation is being run from a laptop, set the laptop up with its back facing into the training room so that the screen is only visible to the trainer. A quick glance at the screen will confirm the progress of the PowerPoint presentation without the need to turn your back on the group.

Know what is coming next

Compare the two following examples:

Trainer number one

The trainer moves the PowerPoint presentation on, turns to face the screen reads the bullet point out and then begins to expand on it, turning back towards their respective audience as they do.

Trainer number two

The trainer imparts some knowledge maintaining eye contact across the group. As they are nearing the end of the point they move the PowerPoint presentation forward to reveal a brief bullet point which reinforces what has just been said.

The difference in style between the two trainers is minor yet the impact is hugely significant.

With trainer number one, the order of presentation is often:

1. Trainer clicks button
2. Trainer looks at screen
3. Bullet appears on screen
4. Trainer breathes a sigh of relief and reads the bullet out loud
5. Trainer says "that's right...." And describes the information

No, no, no!

It's your presentation. You designed it. If you cannot be bothered to practise and learn its content, why should the participants?

Trainer number two appears far more professional. It is evident that they have prepared well for the training session and they fully understand what they are talking about. They know the presentation inside and out. The manner in which they present information is slick and impressive.

The order should be:

1. Trainer describes or discusses an important piece of information
2. Trainer clicks button

3. Bullet reinforcing the message appears on the screen
4. Participants think "Wow, this guy really knows their stuff!"

You should always know what it going to appear on the screen *before* it appears.

Where possible – CHEAT!

You may be running a course for the first time, the course may be newly amended, you may be nervous, have a terrible memory or have too much to remember.

It is important to learn each slide in detail. PowerPoint is at its best when it reinforces the information which is being imparted. The information should first be given by the trainer; this message should then be displayed on the screen in diluted form.

If knowing every dot and comma of your presentation is too much pressure – cheat!

A simple trick is to distil the information included on the PowerPoint presentation down into very brief notes (no more than one piece of A4 paper) and use this as a reminder or prompt. Place it next to the laptop from which the PowerPoint presentation is to be run. In order to progress the presentation use a keyboard key and if required, sneak a peek at what is coming next. If the presentation has been learned, this should only act as a reminder, rather than being relied upon.

Place a glass of water near your notes. If you need a reminder you can take a sip of water and look at your notes.

If the presentation is being run from a laptop, set the laptop up with its back facing into the training room so that the screen is only visible to the trainer. A quick glance at the screen will confirm the progress of the PowerPoint presentation without the need to turn and face the projector screen. Modern versions of PowerPoint have a "presentation mode" which allows the laptop to display the next bullet/image without it showing on the main presentation screen so you will know exactly what will appear next with just a glance.

Know when the screen ends

If there is a set of bullet points on the screen which are to be discussed and introduced separately it is important for the trainer to know which bullet point is the last one. Sometimes it is difficult to memorise the entire list and knowing which one is last will stop the trainer clicking to progress the list and finding it disappearing and moving onto the next screen without the trainer first introducing the transition.

A simple trick is to put a full-stop at the end of the final bullet point. This will not be obvious to onlookers however will signify to the trainer that this is the last bullet point. The list can be drawn to a close and the next screen introduced before it is revealed.

On the rare occasion that someone both notices and raises the fact that only the final bullet has a full-stop, the trainer can be honest and explain the fact that it signifies to them that this is the end of the list and allows them to confidently move onto the next topic. Rather than being met with scorn, this level of professionalism will actually impress those present.

Blank the Screen

> **The only time during a training session when you want to go blank!**

When running a training session it is incredibly important to maintain eye contact with the group. Whilst ever information remains on the screen, people will look at it. This will of course inhibit your ability to maintain eye contact. When you want to divert attention back to yourself and gain the full attention of the group, blank the screen.

> **This is singularly one of the most effective strategies when employing PowerPoint as a presentation medium and the mark of a truly professional trainer**

When in PowerPoint's slideshow mode, press the "B" key. The screen will go blank. When you want the screen to come back on press the "B" key again, it will return to the position at which you left it. If you are presenting on to a white screen and would prefer, press the "W" key and the screen will go white. Again, to return to the presentation we re-press the "W". You will use the "B" key most often though.

Employing the "B" key in such a way will redirect all eyes, and attention, back to the trainer.

Use of the "B" key will also allow you to utilise more of the training area. In the training arena there is no bigger faux pas than walking in front of a projector screen, the trainer's body then being displayed in silhouette. In blanking the screen, the trainer is now able to walk in front of it and utilise other delivery media such as the flip chart or just create movement to maintain interest and attention.

Know the keyboard

There are many ways to navigate within a PowerPoint presentation.

Practising will reap dividends when PowerPoint is then employed.

In brief, the PowerPoint presentation can be moved on using the left click on the mouse, the "page down" button, the "enter" key or either the right or down arrow keys. By far the best method of moving the PowerPoint presentation on is to hit the **"space"** bar. It is the biggest key on the computer so shouldn't need to be looked for which should make it easier to use than any other key.

The presentation can be moved backwards by pressing the "page up" button, either the up or left arrow keys or by right clicking the mouse and selecting previous. The back space button proves convenient as it is larger than most and just above the enter key.

Presentation navigation

It is possible to move forwards and backwards through a presentation using the keys highlighted above. Whilst still employing the keys as above it is also possible to jump to any slide in the presentation. Simply input the number of the slide then press enter.

So, if you want to move to slide 32, simply type 32 and press enter. The presentation will now move to the top of slide 32.

Use the Hard Drive

Try to avoid falling foul of the vagaries of the internet. When possible, run all presentations from the hard drive rather than via the internet as it will run more smoothly.

Maintain a consistent look

Maintain consistent use of slide transitions and builds. As mentioned, less is more and simplicity is best. There are many different builds and transitions, it is not necessary to use all of them. In fact, slick and impressive presentations rely on only one may be two throughout.

Also maintain a consistent use of font types and sizes.

If the slides have headings, ensure they are in the same place on every side. Any deviation will cause the headings to jump as you move from slide to slide.

One way of achieving this is to use the slide Master.

Another is to copy the heading from one slide and paste it on the next. It will automatically be pasted in exactly the same place on the new side. At this point simply overtype this new heading with the relevant title/heading. Now as the presentation progresses from slide to slide, the headings on each slide will be shown in exactly the same place. This will facilitate a smooth transition between slides.

Use of the mouse pointer

If mouse clicks are to be used rather than keyboard strokes to move the presentation on, it is important to keep the mouse's arrow off-screen. It is both off-putting to see the mouse arrow simply hanging onscreen when the presentation is progressing.

If required it is possible to use the mouse arrow as a pointer to direct attention on screen. Pressing "ALT P" turns the mouse pointer into a pen which can be used to write on-screen. Again, when the mouse pointer is not being used, move it off-screen.

Spelling and grammar

Employ spell-check however don't rely on it. Spell-check will only pick-out and correct spelling mistakes, it won't point out incorrect words. Have an independent party provide a "sanity" check by working through the presentation.

Setting up the presentation

Always have the presentation setup prior to the participant's arrival, either at the beginning of the day or during a break.

If a list of the participants names is available use PowerPoint to welcome them. Have an introductory side of the beginning of the presentation:

ABC Consulting welcomes:

Alan Brown

Joe Average

Jim Green

……. and so on, listing each of the participants.

The reaction you will get when a participant sees their name on screen can be quite incredible and it wreaks of professionalism

Moving between Presentations

If there is to be more than one presentation in use, opened them all and use "ALT TAB" to move between the presentations. When using "ALT TAB", the order in which the computer scrolls through the presentations is the order in which they were last viewed. As such, if it is required to switch back and forth between two presentations, holding ALT and then pressing TAB once will go back to the previous presentation.

Try to run videos directly within PowerPoint. Moving to a video player with buttons and a scrubber bar is unprofessional. Embedding the video within your presentation means that simply clicking the link will launch the video on the existing slide.

Opening another presentation

If it is required to move between presentations where "ALT TAB" cannot be used or if a new presentation is to be opened, where possible, cover the projector. Use a piece of folded card (a name card works well) and ensure that the image is no-longer being projected. It appears very unprofessional to come out of one presentation and search or move through files in full view of the group. Covering the projector appears more professional and slick. It is better that the group look at a blank screen than watch the trainer navigate around their own system.

Screen-Saver

It is possible that the laptop from which the training presentation is to be run will have a screen-saver set. The screen-saver is set-up to activate after the laptop has sat idle for a set period of time and produces a message of some description, invariably bouncing randomly across the screen.

It is very off-putting if the screen-saver activates part-way through a training session. It is distracting for the participants and demonstrates poor technique on behalf of the training professional.

The screen-saver can be de-activated or the time-delay increased to mitigate this occurrence. This can be achieved by accessing the display tab within the control panel.

Ending the presentation

Leave some blank sides at the end of the presentation to remove the chance of PowerPoint ending the presentation by mistake.

Flipchart

The flip chart is probably the most popular training aid and its flexibility, availability and versatility explain why it has stood the test of time. It is easy to utilise and portable so can be used anywhere and there is generally at least one flip chart available in most training and meeting rooms.

A flip chart can be used in many different ways at almost any point during the course.

Whilst it is simple to employ, some general tips will help achieve the maximum benefit from its use.

Positioning the Flip chart

If just one flip chart is to be used ensure it is on the right-hand side of the room (from the participant point of view). This will ensure that the trainer will always be stood to the left of it.

Face the group

Do not talk to the flip chart. It is very difficult, if not impossible, to write on the flip chart pad and still face the audience, so when writing on the flip chart, do not talk. A moment's silence is preferable to talking with your back to the group.

Take your time

When writing on the flip chart, face the flip chart and take as long as necessary. This will ensure that the writing is neat and written in a straight line. When not writing, return to the side of the flip chart and face the group.

Positioning

Consider where to stand. Always stand the left of the flip chart. As with the projector screen, the human brain find it easier to absorb information given from somebody stood to the left of a visual aid.

"Hugging" the flip chart

Avoid the temptation to stand behind flip chart. Allowing the flip chart to obscure any part of the body is a sign of nerves. When we are nervous we try to protect ourselves by covering up our torso. Another sign of nerves is to "hug" the flip chart, extending one arm behind the flip chart holding on to the opposite end.

Writing

When using a flip chart print in large letters so that everyone else in the room can make out what is written. Use different coloured wide-tipped pens or large markers to create bold writing.

Obtain a selection of thick tipped marker pens. Use these to create boxes and Borders and to add bullet points to delineate items on the page.

Avoid putting too much information on each page and leave large areas of white space, this will make each page easier to read.

Prepared pages

If any of the flip chart pages are to be prepared in advance leave at least one blank page in between each prepared page. This will stop the prepared page showing through and extra details audience comments can be added without having to flick back and forth through the pad.

Notes and prompts

If necessary it is possible to add notes to the flip chart in a very light HB pencil. If written very small and placed in the top left corner of the flip chart, almost under the fold, it would be possible for the trainer to read and remain invisible to the rest of the group.

Turning the page

When moving the training session on to a new topic, turn to the next blank page of the flip chart pad. Attention will automatically be diverted back to the trainer.

Agenda

The agenda for the course, day or individual session works very well when placed on a flip chart. Unlike PowerPoint or any other medium, the flip chart can be kept and stuck to the wall. This has several benefits. The trainer can use it as a prompt for the sessions running order, the participants can use it to orientate themselves during the day and ticking off sections as they are completed acts as a good motivator.

Post the flip

Relevant information can be stuck to the walls around the training room and offer reinforcement of key points throughout course.

A good technique is to post the participants personal objectives around the room on Flip chart paper. It offers a constant reminder of what they would like to take from the course. It builds confidence as they mentally "tick off" what they have achieved and can be used at the end of the course to confirm attainment of their own, as well as the courses objectives.

Welcome note

When participants first enter the room the flip chart should be blank or contain a greeting. When participants return from breaks, have a motivational quote or saying posted on the flip chart. This can then be kept and placed on the wall.

Disposing of sheets

The flip chart can be used by the participants to present back their ideas or information. When this has been completed either leave the flip charts posted to the wall or place them neatly to one side. Only ever dispose of the participants work at the end of the course when the participants are not present.

Handouts

Issuing handouts at the end of the session or day

If we are lucky, 20% of people will read handouts.

Of course the content is important and should replicate the themes of the day however unless the handouts are to be relied upon later in the course for an exercise, role-play or exam, experience suggests that few will read them.

Even if we work on the premise that some people will not read them it is still important that they positively reflect the session and the course as a whole. Make them look interesting, even from a cursory glance. Make them colourful and consider both the look and feel. Using cheap paper is cost-effective however consider the impact of receiving handouts on paper which has evidently been chosen with care. It doesn't have to be a great deal more expensive to feel it.

An unusual by-product of paying attention to the look and feel of handout is that we might have a positive impact of the number of people who actually read them!

Issuing a handout during a session

Whenever anything is issued to course participants during a session they will read it. While they are reading they are not listening.

If you want them to read only a section or you wish to issue instructions, perhaps for a questionnaire, do this *before* the handout is issued. Whilst this sounds obvious we have all witnessed the disturbance caused when trying to issue instructions and the handout at the same time.

Once you have issued a handout – stop talking. It may be several moments until you are again free to speak. Observe the group as you gradually get eye contact from each member. Wait until you receive it from them all before moving on, it is both polite and good training practise. The group *will* pick up on your professionalism *and* be impressed by it.

Summary

The success of a training programme is greatly affected by the Training Professionals ability to engage and maintain the attention of the participants with a view to sharing ideas and concepts or imparting an important message.

As 93% of communication is derived from the manner in which it is delivered, it is important to adopt the most effective approach and often less is more with simplicity proving the most effective.

The meaning of communication is determined by its recipient and so media should be chosen based on its ability to support the message introduced. The visual aid chosen should complement the session and the trainer. It should support the message rather than actually delivering it.

When employing any form of delivery media the messenger should always remain more important than the visual aid.

Application of very simple techniques will greatly enhance the use of visual aids and help support the training message and delivery of information.

INVALUABLE SESSION ENHANCERS

How to remember names

Mind Accessing

Mind Accessing Stories and Anecdotes

Mind Accessing Attention grabbers

Icebreakers and introductions

Exercises

Quotations

Introduction

The way in which a training course or programme is delivered has a significant effect on its ultimate success.

From setting up the course and creating the right environment to gaining and maintaining the participation of those attending. Employing "The power of yes" and repetition, giving feedback and working the group. In all aspects of course delivery, the application of simple yet effective techniques will contribute greatly to the overall learning experience and therefore the ultimate success of the training and consequently the trainer.

The human brain is like a parachute; it works best when it is open.

Often, apprehension or experience can have a detrimental impact on people's ability to maintain an open mind and without an open mind, little will get through.

The application of Mind-Accessing and rapport building techniques will contribute to the learner's willingness and ability to absorb and enjoy new information, skills and knowledge.

Following are some simple yet effective strategies, the application of which will enhance the learning experience and the impact of the training and therefore ultimately the trainer.

How to remember names

Being able to remember names is a valuable skill, the impact of which can prove extraordinary. It helps build rapport with new contacts, reinforces existing relationships and makes an incredibly good impression on everyone. When employed in the training environment it will propel you to new and impressive heights.

Many people find remembering names very difficult, creating an appreciation of the effort and skill required, making its application all the more impressive.

As most people find remembering the names of the few people around them challenging, if you can remember the names of the ten, fifteen even twenty people on your course, people who you met only hours or minutes before, it is viewed as a remarkable feat.

"But I use name cards!"

There will be many in trainer-land who may well be thinking the obvious – "I use name cards or badges; I don't need to remember names!"

Using name cards or badges does not help you remember people's names, they are encouraging you not to!

If you know there will be a name written in front of each participant, you don't remember their name, you tend to read it when you need it. The issue here is that this is difficult to do this without them seeing you read it. Every time you read their name you are subconsciously telling them that you cannot remember it. That they are not important enough to make a lasting impression. Neither of which is good.

If you travel the extra mile and go out of your way to remember and use people's names it can have a powerful effect:

1. It makes people feel special

2. It demonstrates that you care

3. It is impressive

4. It enhances your credibility

So, there are numerous benefits of remembering names beyond the obvious. It will help build rapport and reinforce existing relationships which is imperative in the training environment. It will also enhance your credibility as it is a skill many people would like to emulate.

Why do we find it so difficult to remember names?

The apprehension caused when meeting people from the first time often inhibits our ability to remember names. This is as a result of a very basic physiological response to stress often referred to as the "fight or flight" response. When placed in a stressful or charged environment we have an immediate physiological response, which is to either run away or defend ourselves. All physiological activities are now geared to support one of these two choices. Our heart beats quickly, passing blood to the physical extremities of our arms and legs.

Adrenaline courses through our body. Any brain function considered unnecessary is curtailed with all focus being placed on the physical rather than mental processes and we act on instinct. In the training environment the stress level is increased as we are not only meeting people for the first-time, we will shortly be facilitating a training programme.

Acknowledging this response will help us to overcome it. Realising what is taking place during these crucial moments will help facilitate the need to implement strategies to compensate and help us process the information we are being given and recall it at will.

General strategies for remembering names

Pay attention

Appreciating the physical and mental effects brought about by the apprehension of meeting people early in the training process will help overcome them.

Take care to pay attention when you first introduce yourself as each of the participants enter the room. Repeat their name out loud as you greet them and shake their hand. If you have misheard they will have the opportunity to correct you and the name begins to be reinforced.

Now repeat their name several times in your mind. A few minutes after you have met them, say his or her name to yourself again. If you cannot remember it, talk to the person again and re-establish their name.

Picture it written on their forehead

Franklin Roosevelt continually amazed his staff by remembering the names of nearly everyone he met. His method was to imagine seeing the name written across the person's forehead. This is a particularly powerful technique if you visualise the name written in your favourite colour of Magic Marker.

Imagine writing the name

Taking the method employed by Franklin Roosevelt a little further, neuro linguistic programming experts suggest getting a feel for what it would be like to write the name by moving your finger in micro-muscle movements as you are seeing the name and saying it to yourself.

Write the name down

Writing down new names is generally a very successful memory technique which does not require a lot of work. This can be completed during the introduction session. Alternatively, write down the new name three times whilst picturing the person's face as soon as possible after first meeting.

Spell the name

Ask how to spell a difficult name or see it written down if possible. If you know the spelling of the word and can picture it in your mind, you will remember it better.

Use it frequently

Try to use the name three or four times during your early conversations. Then employ it during your interactions throughout the training course. This will have several positive effects. It will increase rapport with the individual (somebody remembering your name has a profound impact) as well as helping you remember it. Others will also recognise your ability to remember and use names which will help you appear relaxed, genuine and confident.

Use a contacts file

Top sales representatives as well as great trainers keep a record of new contact names and information, including where and when they met and personal information such as spouse and children's names. Review it when you will again be in contact with these individuals.

Training specific strategies for remembering names

Review the course attendance details

Before the course commences, review the information on the attendees. Having read all of the information, remove all the extraneous data leaving only the participant names on an otherwise clean page. Increase the size of the names and print that page. Familiarise yourself with the names of those who will be attending this course, memorising as many as you can.

By familiarising yourself with the names beforehand, you set up a kind of cognitive dissonance. If you know there are two David's in the group you can concentrate on finding them and remembering what they look like. Under this procedure those with unusual names become easier to remember so you will probably not need to focus on these too much.

Map the room

Before the course begins, draw a plan of the seating arrangement on a clean piece of paper indicating where each chair is positioned. As the participants take their seats write down the names you can remember against the corresponding chair. This can be done gradually as the participants will sometimes hang their coats over the back of the chair all place their folder/case on the table where they intended to sit.

When you complete the course introductions you can fill in the spaces where you have not previously been able to allocate a name.

The territorial nature of the participants will mean that almost without fail, unless you do something to change the environment, they will inevitably keep the same chair throughout the entirety of the course.

This plan becomes your "comfort blanket". You shouldn't need it if you employ some fairly simple memory techniques however having it available as a reference point if you do happen to forget someone's name at any point during the course will help breed confidence in your own abilities. It is like working with a safety net.

Personal introductions

During the personal introductions session, write down the participants name and the personal details divulged. Write these down in the order in which the participants are sitting, from left to right. You now have a reference point of the seating plan should you require it at any point. You also have some important person information about each of the participants which you can refer back to during the course. This can be incorporated into your "contacts" file for future reference.

Personal objectives

One method of creating a seating plan is to record the participant's personal objectives on a flip chart early on in the course. Working in a logical sequence (generally from left to right), write the participant's name on the flip chart and record their personal objectives just underneath. Repeat this process for the whole group. You will probably get between two and three participants per page. Post these on the wall so that they reflect the order in which the participants are sitting. Again, due to the territorial nature of the participants they will only change this order if you instigate it. You now have a list of the participant's names in the order in which they are seated should you need a reference point at any time.

Name cards

During meetings or training sessions one accepted convention is to use name cards. They are certainly handy where none of the participants know each other. In these circumstances they actually prove as beneficial to those present as they do to you as a trainer. Remember, those attending the course might not be as good at remembering names as you!

Even if you choose to employ name cards, it will prove beneficial not to rely on them to remember names. Apply any of the strategies mentioned previously. You can then maintain eye contact throughout the sessions. As discussed, the need to glance down and read somebody's name during a session is off-putting and can inhibit the rapport building process. If you actively remember the names you can also employ them during syndicate work and breaks where the name cards are not present.

If the course attendees already know each other using name cards would be like telling them that you are no good at remembering names and they are not important enough for to you to try. Again, employ the practices discussed rather than name cards and reap the positive benefits.

Remembering names

Remembering names is one of those skills which is not missed if it isn't their yet noticed when it is. As such, it is easy to get away with simple strategies like the application name cards. There use is now so prevalent most people simply won't notice. When you negate the need to use name cards the participants will notice. It will be appreciated and your reputation will be taken to new levels.

Mind Accessing

Mind Accessing involves breaking down mental barriers helping us engage our respective audiences.

The following are a collection of stories and anecdotes, exercises and energisers which will add flavour and impact to any training session or course.

These have been taken from the book:

"Tales for the Training Room" also by Jimmy Miller

"Tales for the Training Room" is a collection of stories, anecdotes, quotations, energisers and exercises which have been gathered over a training career spanning well over a decade.

They can be used to Gain Attention, Maintain Interest, Create Desire, Reinforce your information and message, Offer reassurance or Build rapport.

It forms an invaluable resource for those delivering talks, speeches, lectures, workshops, presentations and training courses.

Mind Accessing Stories and Anecdotes

Time Management

Following is a great way of introducing the concept of Time Management

One day, an expert in time management was speaking to a group of business students. To drive home the point he used a very clever illustration that should stick in minds of the students.

As he stood in front of the group he said:

"Okay, time for a quiz" and pulled out a one-gallon, wide-mouth Mason jar, setting it on the table in front of him. He also produced about a dozen fist-sized rocks and carefully placed them, one at a time, into the jar.

When the jar was filled to the top and no more rocks would fit inside, he asked:

"Is this jar full?" Everyone in the class yelled, "Yes."

The time management expert replied, "Really?" He reached under the table and pulled out a bucket of gravel. He dumped some gravel in and shook the jar causing pieces of gravel to work themselves down into the spaces between the big rocks. He then asked the group once more:

"Is the jar full?" By this time the class was on to him.

"Probably not," one of them answered.

"Good!" he replied.

He reached under the table and brought out a bucket of sand. He started scooping the sand into the jar and it went into all of the spaces left between the rocks and the gravel. Once more he asked:

"Is this jar full?"

"No!" the class shouted. Once again he said, "Good." Then he grabbed a jug of water and began to pour it into the jar until it was filled to the brim. He then looked at the class and asked:

"What is the point of this illustration?"

One eager beaver raised his hand and said, "The point is, no matter how full your schedule is, if you try really hard you can always fit some more things in it!"
"No," the speaker replied, "that's not the point."

"The truth which this illustration teaches us is, if you don't put the big rocks in first, you'll never get them in at all. What are the 'big rocks' in your life, time with loved ones, your faith, your education, your dreams, a worthy cause, teaching or mentoring others? Remember to put these BIG ROCKS in first or you'll never get them in at all. So, tonight, or in the morning, when you are reflecting on this short story, ask yourself this question, 'What are the 'big rocks' in my life?' Then, put those in your jar first."

Marketing Opportunity

A large shoe manufacturer looked to increase profits and recognised that a key to its success was to increase volume. With this in mind its business strategy was to expand its market place into countries with whom they currently had no dealings.

The company sent two executives to a remote region of a third-word country to study the prospects for business expansion.

Looking to report back to the board of directors an update report was requested. Two emails were subsequently received:

One executive confirmed the following:

'No opportunities for expansion - no one wears shoes.'

The other email reads:

'They have no shoes - tremendous business opportunity.'

In case of rain

Where the intention is to up-lift the participants the following focuses on belief, faith and total commitment:

The fields were parched and brown from lack of rain. The crops lay wilting from thirst.

People were anxious and irritable as they searched the sky for any sign of relief. Days turned into arid weeks yet no rain came.

The ministers of the local churches gathered together and called for an hour of prayer on the town square the following Saturday. They requested that everyone bring on object of faith for inspiration.

At high noon on the appointed Saturday the townspeople turned out en masse, filling the square with anxious faces and hopeful hearts. The ministers were touched to see the variety of objects clutched in prayerful hands ranging from holy books and crosses to rosaries.

When the hour ended and as if on magical command, a soft rain began to fall. Cheers swept the crowd as they held their treasured objects high in gratitude and praise.

From the middle of the crowd one faith symbol seemed to overshadow all the others.

A small nine-year old child had brought an umbrella.

The Final Exam

The following is a lovely story which can be used when you want to encourage self-belief or motivation:

A professor stood before his class of 20 senior organic biology students, about to hand out the final exam.

"I want to say that it's been a pleasure teaching you all. I know you've all worked extremely hard and many of you are off to medical school after the summer. So that no one gets their GP messed up because they might have been celebrating a bit too much this week, anyone who would like to opt out of the final exam today will receive a "B" for the course."

There was much rejoicing amongst the class as students got up, passed by the professor to thank him and sign out on his offer. As the last taker left the room, the professor looked out over the handful of remaining students and asked, "Anyone else? This is your last chance."

One final student rose up and took the offer. The professor closed the door and took attendance of those students remaining.

"I'm glad to see you believe in yourself." he said. "You all have A's."

The story can be completed by adding that many people are willing to accept being average, average being best of the worst or the worst of the best. It feels good to amongst winners.

You have two choices

Again, the following is a story which engenders positivity and self-belief. It inspires the individual to take control of their own thought processes, own choices and ultimately their life:

Jerry is the manager of a restaurant. He is always in a good mood. Many of the workers at his restaurant would quit when he changed jobs, following him around from restaurant to restaurant.

Why?

Jerry was a natural motivator. If an employee was having a bad day Jerry was always there, telling the employee how to look on the positive side of the situation. People would say "I don't get it. No one can be that positive. No one can be in a good mood all of the time." Jerry would reply, "Each morning I wake up and say to myself, Jerry, you have two choices today. You can choose to be in a good mood or you can choose to be in a bad one. I always choose to be in a good mood.

Each time something bad happens I can choose to be a victim or I can choose to learn from it. I always choose to learn from it.

Every time someone comes to me complaining, I can choose to accept their complaining or I can point out the positive side of life. I always choose the positive side of life."

"It's not always that easy" they would say. "Yes, it is" Jerry would reply. "Life is a series of choices.

You choose how you react to situations.
You choose how people will affect your mood.
You choose to be in a good mood or a bad one.
It's your choice how you live your life."

Several years later Jerry's restaurant was robbed. While he was trying to open the safe, he struggled to input the combination. The robbers panicked and shot him.

Luckily Jerry was found quickly and rushed to hospital. Jerry underwent 18 hours of surgery and spent weeks in intensive care.

Surely, even Jerry couldn't see the positive side in this situation.

Months later Jerry was asked about the robbery. "The first thing that went through my mind was that I should have locked the back door! Then, after they shot me, as I lay on the floor bleeding, I remembered that I had two choices.
I could choose to die or I could choose to live. I chose to live.

The paramedics were great. They kept telling me I was going to be fine. When they wheeled me into the emergency room and I saw the expression on the doctor's faces I got really scared. Their eyes said that I was a dead man.

There was a big nurse shouting questions at me. She asked if I were allergic to anything. Yes I replied. The doctors and nurses stopped working and waited for my reply.

I took a deep breath and said...bullets! Over their laughter I told them I am choosing to live. Please operate on me as if I'm alive, not dead!

Jerry lived thanks to the skills of the doctors and nurses and his amazing attitude. We can learn a lot from him. Every day you have the choice to either enjoy your life or hate it. The only thing that is truly yours, the thing that no one can take away from you is your attitude. Other people can only control it if you let them.

Your attitude affects how you live your life so protect it!

The Red Arrows

This is an incredible story however it does make reference to a funeral. Anyone who has experienced this, whether recently or not will appreciate what a terribly emotive subject this is. It may conjure up some very strong feelings. If it is to be used it is worth prefacing it by pointing out that the story mentions a funeral by way of a warning. Explain that the message is something you wish to share and ask for the participant's indulgence.

A man was invited to the funeral of his uncle. He had always talked at length and with great affection about his uncle who had lived an interesting life. He had a varied career taking him to every corner of the globe. If his life was in a book we would probably read it if it was on film I think we'd enjoy watching it.

He was in the merchant Navy and then worked in several areas of the armed forces. In fact, the last 17 years he had spent working as an engineer for the red arrows. We can only imagine the things he would have experienced and the places he visited as a result.

At a predetermined time the grieving family asked everybody present to step outside. They looked to the sky and were rewarded with the most amazing spectacle, as a mark of respect the red arrows performed a flyby.

As those present looked on and took in the scene, it became apparent that something was not quite right. The Red Arrows are the UK's premiere display team and most of the people had seen them at some time before. This time however, something was different.

As the planes flew overhead in perfect formation the difference gradually dawned on the crowd and tears began to flow openly.

What did they notice?
One of the planes in the formation was quite clearly missing.

Which one?
The one he worked would have been working on.

Not only did the display team want to show their respect. They also wanted to demonstrate their loss.

They would miss him.
The most profound things in life are often those that are missing. The fact is in life; we often only notice things when they're *not* there.

For example, the only time we really talk about service is when it is *missing*!!!

An introduction for Insurance , Cars or Children

Generally, the sale of insurance would be considered a fairly dry topic however no topic needs to be dry. All training, irrespective of the content can be interesting and engaging. In fact, all training should be interesting and engaging if it is to be effective.

The following story introduces the concept of insurance in a light-hearted way.

A car was parked in a rough area which was renowned for gangs of youths who would roam the streets causing trouble. Unfortunately, the car was broken into. The thieves smashed the driver's side window, stealing the CD player and some personal items.

The owner was required to complete an insurance claim form.

The form kept referring to the "incident" which the owner thought rather belittled the event. As most claims occur as the result of an accident, the form required a great deal of information including a diagram and description of the "incident". The owner persisted and completed all areas of the form.

The final question asked:
"Who, in your opinion, is at fault for this incident?"

The owner responded:
"Frankly, I blame the parents!"

Mind Accessing Attention grabbers

Mind-accessing should be something which is constantly applied, its application permeating into to all aspects of training design and delivery.

It may occasionally be necessary to open the mind using a short presentation, to literally grab the participant's attention before entering into a specific session.

Following are examples of attention grabbing presentations which can be used to gain the interest of the participants and firm up their commitment to learning:

5. Think of a number (Grey elephant in Denmark)

6. A Simple card trick

7. Air traffic controller

8. Attitude

9. Optimist/pessimist – thinking about what you want rather than what you don't want

10. Newton's 3rd Law

1. <u>Think Of A Number</u>

Instruction:

Don't tell me what it is…. everyone think of a number between 1 and 9.

You will be thinking of a one digit number. Multiply it by 9.

You should now be thinking of a two digit number. Add the two digits together.

You should now be thinking of a one digit number…..just to make sure, subtract 5.

You should now definitely be thinking of a one digit number.

Okay, we are now going to translate this number into a letter using a very simple code. If you are thinking of the number 1, this will become the letter "A" as this is the first letter of the alphabet. If you are thinking of the number 2 this will be "B", 3 becomes "C", 4 would be "D and so one.

Everyone thinking of a letter? Great.

Now, think of a country beginning with that letter, remember the country.

Take the second letter of the country and think of an animal that you may find in a zoo that starts with this letter.

What colour is your animal?

"Grey" will be the dubious responses

So, who is thinking of A GREY ELEPHANT IN DENMARK??

Reveal this picture on or prepared flip chart or PowerPoint slide

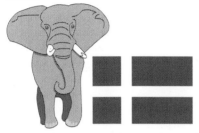

Grey elephant in Denmark

This is a great introduction for any kind of process or sales training involving a specific track. A simple set of steps leads to a predetermined destination.

2. <u>A Simple Card Trick</u>

Inform the participants that you have the ability to read their minds.

Via PowerPoint or on a prepared flip, display the following Playing Cards:

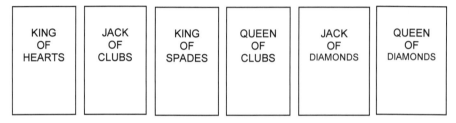

Ask the participants to mentally choose a card.

Tell them "Keep it a secret. Do not tell anyone which card you have chosen."

"Now, focus on the card. Staring intently at the card, concentrate really hard. Focus. Focus. Okay, I know which card you have chosen. Remember the card you chose. Now I will make your card disappear!"

Now display the following cards:

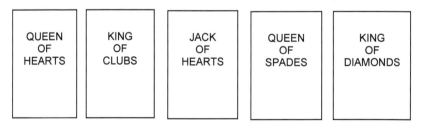

Now ask – "Did it go?"

Stand back and enjoy the looks of amazement.

This is a form of introduction is great for any kind of training involving a specific track or process. Following a simple set of steps can bring about an amazing response.

3. Air traffic controller

This can be used to reinforce the need for training and development and allow the participants to feel justified in attending the training programme and working hard. It compares experience and training. More importantly it reinforces the fact that the two are not mutually exclusive – **you can have both!!**

Put up a picture of an Air Traffic Controller

Instruction:

Ask: What is he/she doing for a living?

Anticipated response: Air Traffic Controller

Ask: Who has any programmes about the role or read any articles?

Anticipated response: Positive response

Ask: What kind of pressure are they
under?

Anticipated response: A great deal

Ask: Why is that?

Anticipated response: Due to the nature of the role

Ask: What are the implications of them making a mistake?

Anticipated response: Catastrophic

State: It is a highly stressful job which requires the talents of highly skilled and experienced individuals.

Let's say this individual has 20 years' experience

Change the subject slightly:

Ask: Who has been on holiday?

Anticipated response: Everyone

Ask: flew?   When you went on holiday, who

Anticipated response: Most

Ask: Yes, we are seeing this more and more. Who has been on more than one holiday in any one year?

Anticipated response: Everyone

Ask: Again, we are seeing this more and more. How often do both of these holidays require flights?

Anticipated response: Again, most

State:

This is the position we expect nowadays. The world is getting smaller. More and more people are flying more and more often. This seems very obvious however it hasn't always been this way. If we look back 20 years as an example there simply weren't as many planes in the sky and fewer people thought to take advantage of those that were.

Return to the Air Traffic Controller:

Returning to this Air Traffic Controller, they started their role 20 years ago. Gradually over these two decades this role has changed. More and more planes require their expertise more and more often and we know the implications of them making a mistake!

Let's consider two different scenarios, *both* involving this *same* Air Traffic Controller:

Position 1:

They started their role 20 years ago and gradually over the last 20 years they have amassed a great deal of really good experience.

Position 2:

This is the same person. They started their role 20 years ago and gradually over the last 20 years they have amassed the same really good experience. On top of that though, they originally went on a two-week residential training course where they were taught everything they needed to know about their job role. Then, gradually over the 20 years they have received regular updates, coaching, mentoring, training and development. They have been encouraged to continually reinforce and update their skills as times, and therefore their job-role, has changed. In fact the last course they attended was (describe the course you are about to run e.g. - a three day residential training course in Leeds) which helped them reinforce and update their skills in line with industry changes *and you are getting on a plane* ....

.... Of these two scenarios, which one would you rather have controlling the destiny of it?

(The participants will like the fact that you are being honest and it will appear less contrived if you admit why you are using this story!)
So **Continue:**

Now I wouldn't embarrass you for an answer however guess where I am going with this.

That's right, I'm justifying why I am here today. Hopefully you will recognise the importance of being here as well.

The fact is that when *we* are customers *we* prefer dealing with well trained, professional people. *Our customers are no different*!

Go on to describe what they will take from the course

4. __ATTITUDE__

This is used to reinforce the importance of an individual's attitude to attaining the results they want.

ASK: How important is attitude to …… (use the topic to be covered by the training)…..?

Anticipated response: Imperative

STATE: That's right, let's have a look:

ASK: How do you spell attitude?

Anticipated response: A-T-T-I-T-U-D-E

INSTRUCTION:

Write the word attitude vertically down a Flip chart.

```
A

T

T

I
T

U

D

E
```

NOW STATE:

We will just convert the word into numbers using a very simple code. "A" is the first letter of the alphabet so this will be "1"

Write this on the Flip chart to the right of the "A".

NOW ASK:

So where does "T" fall in the alphabet?

Anticipated response: 20

Add this to the flip chart and continue until the flip chart has the correct numbers alongside each letter:

A	1
T	20
T	20
I	9
T	20
U	21
D	4
E	5

Now, pointing to each number in turn ask what is "1" add "20" add "20" add "9" ..... and so on until you reach the final number ... add "5" and you have the desired answer "100"

Add this figure to the Flip chart:

A	1
T	20
T	20
I	9
T	20
U	21
D	4
E	<u>5</u>
	<u>100</u>

STATE:

That's right. Attitude is 100% in all that we do…….

If it is important to lighten the mood **ASK**:

Do you know what is even more incredible than that?…… The fact that someone sat down and worked that out!

Then **ADD**:

**It doesn't stop it being true!**

5. Optimist/Pessimist

A more positive approach to training will enhance the course as a whole, the participants experience and the likelihood of the content being applied on return to the work environment.

Continuing the importance of attitude, the distinction between Optimist and Pessimist can be likened to approaching things in a positive or negative manner.

It is important to emphasise the fact that there is no right or wrong approach in life. What we want to consider is how each approach will affect the results we may attain.

Definition Exercise:

First, have the participants define the Optimist and the Pessimist.

Anticipated response:

The likely responses will refer to a positive or negative approach.

The effect of attitude: (Place this quote on Flip chart or PowerPoint)

> *"The human brain is like a magnet. We are drawn to that which we think about"*

Cater for the Pessimists:

Simply emphasising the benefits of a positive approach will turn off those who have a more negative approach. It is important to validate their approach whilst leaning towards a positive mental approach.

Explain that Pessimism has its advantages. If we were in a plane which flying rather low and heading towards a mountain, the last thing we would want is an overly-optimistic pilot!!

Now go on to explain that: *The human brain is like a magnet. We are drawn to that which we think about*

If we have a more positive approach we are more likely to be successful. We will also have a better time!!

6. <u>Newton's 3rd Law</u>

People generally know more than they think they know. The real trick is getting them to know it and drawing it out.

<u>Newton's 3rd Law</u>

Newton's 3rd Law states:

Every action has an equal and opposite re-action

This is a great exercise.

Whilst most participants may think they don't know how to do "it", they will probably be able to figure out how *not* to do "it".

It does not matter what the "it" is. This will of course vary and depend on where and when this exercise is used.

The exercise:

Explain the main topic for the session, for example "Presentation Skills".

Explain that we will be looking at how to do great presentations; first we will consider what a bad one would look like:

Split into groups and have them create and then deliver a "terrible" presentation. The other groups will offer a critique.

Put up Newton's 3rd Law.

Now point out that for every action there is an equal and opposite re-action,

So, what would be the opposite of crappy? This is the solution:

Icebreakers and introductions

Apprehension is brought about when individuals are thrust together as a group of people in a shared experience. Successful training is rarely an individual effort. If there is no interaction, this actually becomes more of a presentation. Interaction with people we do not know can be uncomfortable so the training must first encourage introductions of some sort.

No one should be made to feel uncomfortable on a training course. Most people have experienced the "rep from hell" on their annual holiday. They have spent many months saving for this once a year experience of rest and relaxation and then dare not venture too close to the stage for fear of being physically dragged up and ritualistically humiliated!

This fear and apprehension is often brought onto a training course and demonstrated with a roll of the eyes or groan as soon as introductions are mentioned.

So, we must consider the outcome first. What are we aiming to get out of the course?

If it is a one-day "blast", then short introductions will probably suffice. These are less time-consuming and more lengthy introductions may create ill feeling.

If the course is slightly longer, or one where lots of group work will be required, the introductions or icebreaker can help the participants to get to know each other.

Following are a selection of Icebreakers and Introduction exercises:

1. *Playing Cards*
2. *Survival Exercise*
3. *Coat of Arms*
4. *Human Web*
5. *Jigsaw Game*
6. *I've always done it that way*
7. *Magic Paper Circle Game*
8. *Secret Agent*
9. *Tennis Balls*
10. *10% Stretch*
11. *Guest Speaker Introduction*
12. *I'm glad I'm here*

1. Playing Cards

Requirements
One deck of cards per team
Watch with a second hand
One table per team
Flipchart, clearly visible to all teams (more than 1 flipchart may be required)

Running The Exercise
Prepare flipchart(s) with the following list:

A 2 10 6 J 4 7 K 3 9 5 Q 8 (each suit)

Instruction:

The object is to arrange the playing cards in a pack in suits in the order shown on the flipchart. Time will be given to plan how you will undertake the exercise (allow 4 minutes). At the end of the planning time you will be asked to commit to a time i.e. how long it will take you as a team to arrange and display the cards starting with the pack (shuffled) in the hands of one member of the group. (Encourage competition between the groups).

There is one rule - you must all take part.

Notes:

Several rounds can be run depending on time with people swapping from group to group at either the end of an action phase or even during.

At some point, if required, add the information that the record time is 23 seconds. Look at their faces.

Debrief
Did they have an honest expectation of their performance?
How did the team work?
How did the team work when the members were swapped? -
Did the new addition to the team feel a part of it immediately?
How were you motivated? Did you use your time effectively?

2. <u>Plane Crash - Survival Exercise</u>

Requirements
Strong tables
Coloured masking tape

Running the Exercise
Arrange two tables alongside each other leaving a gap of approximately 1/2 metre (may need more tables depending on number of attendees).

Place the masking tape about 5 inches in on the table and arrange for the attendees to stand between the masking tape.

Instruction:

You are the only survivors of a plane crash, which crashed in a South American jungle. You are currently being hunted down by the enemy and you have all remained together. You now have to cross a deadly crocodile/alligator infested swamp. They only way to cross the swamp is by going across a bridge. Unfortunately the bridge is on its last legs and can therefore only be crossed one at a time.

In order to be fair as to who crosses the bridge first it has been decided that you will cross the bridge in order of date of birth with the youngest going first.

The enemy are getting closer. You do not want to disturbing the crocodiles or alligators and so you are not able to communicate verbally and cannot cross over the masking tape.

Debrief

How did the team communicate?

Was there a leader who organised the team or was it a little chaotic?

A leader is essential in this type of situation - somebody needs to take control.

Was everybody involved, what was the body language telling you?

3. <u>Coat of Arms</u>

Requirements
Coloured pens
Flipchart paper

Running the Exercise
Draw a demonstration shield on the Flipchart paper. Split into 5 areas:

Spare time and Activities
Big Achievement
A Secret
Your Job
Your personal Motto

Distribute paper and pens

Instruction:

Draw a shield on a piece of flip chart paper, similar to the shield shown on the Flipchart.

In each segment, draw pictures to represent the aspect of your life as labelled. You will be asked to present your shield to the group and explain your drawings.

4. <u>The Human Spider Web</u>

Requirements
None

Running The Exercise
Ask the group(s) to stand in a small circle.

Instruction:

Extend your left hand across the circle and grasp the right hand of person who is approximately opposite. Now extend your right hand across the circle and grasp the left hand of another individual.

Your task is to unravel the spider web of interlocking arms without letting go of anyone's hands.

NB: If there is just one team, inform them that they will be timed (as a way to place pressure on them). If there are several groups, tell them they will be competing with each other to see who finishes the task first.

Debrief
What was you first thought when you heard the nature of the task?
What member behaviours detracted (or could detract) from the group's success in achieving this goal?
What learning can we take forward from this to our workplace?

5. Jigsaw Game

Requirements:
Children's jigsaws with between 6 - 12 pieces, one per team.
Optional small prize (i.e. fun size sweets etc.)

Running The Exercise
Before the attendees arrive, tip the jigsaws out and mix some pieces around between jigsaws so that the pieces left in each puzzle will not make up a correct picture. Do not inform them of this. Place each *new* jigsaw into a small plastic bag ready for distribution.

Instruction:

You are to undertake a child's jigsaw of anything between 6 and 12 pieces.

Ask each group how long they think it will take them to put the jigsaw together.

The first group to fully complete the jigsaw will win a prize.

The jigsaws cannot be tipped out until I start the exercise.

You will need to work as a team to complete the jigsaw.

Start the exercise immediately afterward this instruction.

NB: During the completion of the puzzles, keep shouting out how long they have had in an attempt to get staff to beat the timings pledged.

It won't be long before they will realise that they need to swap pieces from each other's jigsaws to complete the task.

Debrief:

The need to work together to complete tasks - they can't always be completed on their own (i.e. re-cap on facilitators instruction to work as a team to complete the task).How do staff now feel?: happy / relaxed / fun / up for it!! Staff who are feeling this at the start of the day / week will go for it and motivation will be good.

6. I've Always Done It That Way

Requirements:
Jacket/Coat/Cardigan to be worn by attendees.
If all attendees do not have one, use these as observers

Running The Exercise

Ask observers to watch the reactions as you go through exercise.

Instruction: (to all attendees with jackets)

Stand up and remove you jacket. Now put them back on, noting which arm goes in first.

Now, take off your jackets again. Now, put them back on. This time, putting the other arm in first!

Debrief
Ask attendees:
1. How did it feel to reverse your normal pattern of putting on your jacket......?
2. Was it so awkward to do? Ask observers for feedback on reactions.
3. What prevents us from adopting new ways of doing things? How can we make changes without old habits interfering with them?
4. How can we open ourselves to change and accept that there may be equally effective, if not even better ways to accomplish our tasks than we've used before?

7. Magic Paper Circle Game

Requirements
One sheet of A4 paper per team

Running The Exercise
Participants form into teams. Issue each some A4 paper.

Instruction:

Your task is to pass the entire team through a hole in one of these sheets of paper. The hole must be surrounded by unbroken paper, and no other items are to be used.

The first team to achieve this are the winner.

NB: Point out the apparent impossibility on first approaching this task.

If one team has the right idea and the others catch on to the general approach, note this.
If no-one completes the exercise in 5 - 10 minutes, demonstrate the solution; If a team completes this successfully, get them to show the rest what they did.

Solution

1. Fold the paper in two. Make a series of 4 tears, from the folded edge towards the other edge, leaving a clear centimetre of un-torn paper in each case. See below.

Folded edge →

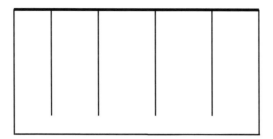

2. Make 3 tears in the opposite direction, between the original tears. Again, leave a clear centimetre at the end.

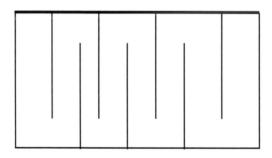

3. Tear along the crease of the three central creased end points. Open out the sheet of paper. It will make a paper ring, plenty big enough to pass a person through.

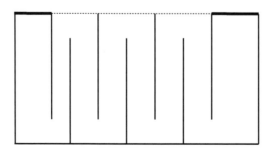

Debrief

Provided the puzzle is solved there's a good physical aspect to getting the team members through the paper.

How did the team manage the task? The initial problem solving could be low energy.

Were they organised or was it chaotic?

Did they think outside the box i.e. look at different ways of doing things - challenging ideas.

NB: If the team do not solve the puzzle, it may be you show them the solution, then have a race to see who can do it the quickest and pass all team members through.

It may be an idea to practice this yourself first so you are confident of the solution.

8. <u>Secret Agent</u>

Requirements
Large area in which to run the exercise

Running The Exercise
Ask all participants to stand in a circle.

Instruction:

Someone in the group is out to get you, they are a "secret agent". Only you know who they are. Now, each of you also has a "bodyguard", who again, only you know the identity of.

Quietly and without pointing or telling anyone, look around and secretly choose who your "secret agent" is for this game.

After everyone seems to have made a selection now select another individual, again quietly and without pointing or telling anyone, who will serve as your "bodyguard".

After everyone has made their choices you are now free to move about the room. You MUST keep your "bodyguard" between you and your "secret agent" at all times.

NB: This can get pretty funny and interesting as people move about. It often turns into utter chaos because of the odd combinations of 'bodyguards' and 'secret agents'.

End the game when you feel like it's over.

9. <u>Tennis Balls</u>

Requirements
5 tennis balls and 1 bin per team.

Running The Exercise
Place a bin for each team on a chair some distance away from a line drawn with tape.

FIRST ROUND:
The team members select who will throw the balls. They have to get 20 balls in the bin within a 3 minute time frame.

Ensure that the bin is far enough away from them **NOT** to achieve this objective.
Generally they will become disheartened by the fact that they cannot achieve their goals.

SECOND ROUND:
The Teams can negotiate the terms of their goals, the position of the chair and bin etc. This time they will make it too easy and become de-motivated.

Debrief
Imposing objectives or goals can be de-motivating
Agreeing objectives or goals is motivating, however, if set too low they can be de-motivating. Agreeing a middle ground is the key to motivating performance improvement.
Support and encouragement from the team keeps spirits and motivation high.

The link into coaching is - get staff to state their goals, areas for improvement get their buy in. Play on their strengths. Give them support, encouragement, feedback, guidance and praise.

NB: THIS IS ALSO VERY EFFECTIVE IF STAFF ARE BLINDFOLDED!!

10. *The 10% Stretch*

Requirements
None

Running The Exercise
Pair the attendees up and ask them to stand to the side of the room, against a wall. Request that one from each pair closes their eyes and extends an arm and reach as high as possible on the wall as he or she can. Ask the second person from the pair to measure approximately how high the person's outstretched fingertips reached.

Now as ask them to keep their eyes closed and ask them to visualise the stretch, *really high, stretching as far as possible (you need to really sell this section!)*.

Now still with their eyes closed, ask them to extend their arm again, by *really stretching*, reach as high as possible. Note how far the fingertips extended this time (it will invariably be farther).

Debrief
Ask them to derive their own conclusion form this exercise.
Ask them to note the effects of a 10% improvement by say a football player, for example - more touches of the ball, more goals, fewer bad shots and bookings etc.
What apprehensions do we have about doing something new or different?
Could our team improve performance in some area by 10% or more? What areas?

N.B. You may find that some attendees will exhibit defensiveness by indicating that they are already working as hard as they can. Without debating their behaviour, simply ask them if they are aware of any other staff in their branch who are not contributing all they possibly can (they'll rarely deny this!!)

11. <u>Guest Speaker Introduction</u>

Requirements:
Information of the guest speaker.

Running The Exercise
Make a list of things you know about the guest speaker on a sheet of paper. Cut up the sheet of paper and distribute pieces to several participants in advance so each has a sentence or two to read or memorise.

When you begin to introduce the guest, state "Our guest is so well known, I'll bet you know more about him/her than I do." Then, on cue, the participants relate something about the speaker's background.

12. I'm Glad I'm Here

Requirements:
None

Running The Exercise
Immediately after your introduction to the course tell the group that you're happy to be there also!! To prove that, go around the room and ask each individual "If you weren't here today, what would you be doing that you're glad you don't have to do?"

Keep the answers light, fast moving and try to add a little humour.

Debrief
Remind staff periodically throughout the day when they are tiring or negative what they could have been doing instead!!!

Energisers

Training courses, whilst rewarding, can prove incredibly draining. During most working days we are offered distractions of all sorts. Unlike most working days, the participants are concentrating for long periods of time. The use of exercises will form a good break however every now and then it may prove beneficial to energise the room.

Changing physiology also changes mindset. The aim of an energiser is to get the heart pumping. Energisers will re-invigorate and re-energise, they will allow people the opportunity to re-focus and offer a total break from the learning experience.

The best energisers are unrelated to the learning and simply form a momentary distraction allowing the participants to return to the course with a renewed vigour.

The following can be used to re-energise participants at any time during a course:

1. Fruit Salad

2. Have you had breakfast?

3. Who am I?

4. Tennis Ball Sequence Game

5. Cow Tails Game

1. <u>Fruit Salad</u>

Requirements:

One chair per participant

Running the Energiser:

Arrange one chair per participant in a circle facing inwards.

Have the participants sit on the chairs.

Stand in the middle.

Instruction:

Point at one of the participants and say "Orange". Then point at the Participant to their left and say "Lemon", turn to the left of them and point at the next labelling them "Orange", next one "Lemon" and so on right around the circle until everyone is either an orange or a lemon.

Next, tell them:

"the object is to be seated. If the person in the middle says "Orange", all the oranges must swap places. If the person in the middle says "Lemon", all the lemons must swap places. If the person in the middle says "Fruit Salad", everyone must swap seats."

Ensure everyone understands

Now, say "Orange"

As the oranges swap seats, quickly sit in one of the free seats. This will now leave one of participants in the centre.

They will now say either Orange, lemon or fruit salad in order to get a seat......and so on.

2. Have you had breakfast?

This is a variation on fruit Salad and runs in a similar way, substituting instructions for fruits.

Requirements:

One chair per participant

Running the Energiser:

Arrange one chair per participant in a circle facing inwards.

Have the participants sit on the chairs.

Stand in the middle.

Instruction:

Explain:

"The object is to be seated. If the person in the middle makes a statement which relates to you, you must swap seats with someone."

For example, if I were to say "Swap seats if you ate breakfast today, if you had breakfast this morning you need to swap seats with someone." Ensure everyone understands

Move straight on and say "So, swap seats if you ate breakfast today!"

As the participants swap seats, quickly sit in one of the free seats. This will now leave one of participants in the centre.

Look at the participant and say "Your turn"

They will now come up with a statement and say "Swap seats if you (Examples follow)" in order to get a seat......and so on.

Examples might be:

Swap seats if you have been on holiday this year
Swap seats if you drive a car
Swap seats if you are married
Swap seats if you play football
Swap seats if you own a pet
Swap seats if you ski
Swap seats if you like Chinese food
Swap seats if you can ride a bike

If necessary, add in your own:

3. Who am I?

Aim:

This can be used simply as an energiser or to learn/reinforce the learning of the participants names.

Requirements:

No specific requirements other than sufficient room to stand in a circle.

Running the Energiser:

Arrange the participant in a circle facing inwards.

Explain to the participants that the aim of the exercise is to help them forget their own name!!

Instruction:

One of the participants will point at another and say *their own* name. The participant pointed at will then, in turn, point to another participant and say **their own** name. This new participant will point to another participant and say **their own** name..........and so on.

NB:

The participants will basically point at someone else and say their own name.

This sounds straight forward however the temptation when they point at someone is to say *that person's* name, rather than *their own*.

Increase the pace and very soon people will begin pointing and saying the other person's name, effectively neglecting to say their own.

Keep going until confusion, and hopefully laughter, reigns.

4. Tennis Ball Sequence Game

Requirements
Tennis balls - number equivalent to the number of participants in the exercise

Running The Exercise
Participants form a circle of a least 6 people (more than one circle may be appropriate depending on the number of participants)

ROUND ONE:

Allocate one tennis ball to each team, irrespective of the size of the team.
Throw one tennis ball to any member of the team. Tell participants to then throw the ball to other members of their team, calling out the name of the person to whom they are throwing the ball (it may therefore be necessary to have a 'name call' at this point). Explain that each person in the team must throw and catch the ball at least once in each round. When the ball has been round everyone once, ask participants to repeat the exercise and to keep throwing the ball round the circle as before.
After a few minutes, introduce further balls and then periodically keep introducing further balls to the exercise. It may become a little chaotic at this point, but fun also!

ROUND TWO:

Stop the exercise and ask the participants to now reverse the process i.e. throw the ball back to the person who originally passed it to them (watch for reactions as you ask them to do this). Let this run for a new minutes then stop.

Debrief
Do they now know the name of a few more of the attendees?
How did the attendees manage the 1st ball?
What were their thoughts when the 2nd, 3rd, 4th..... ball were thrown into the circle?

Did they think they wouldn't cope with them - and did they??
Although we initially think we can't cope with more workloads, we do, once we get used to them, we manage.

We can manage change and it will work.

5. Cow Tails Game

Requirements
Blindfolds - one per team
Cow pictures - one per team
Tails (string) - one per team
Blu-tack

Running The Exercise
This is a variation of 'pin the tail on the donkey', this time with cows.

Split the group into teams of 3-4 people. The object is to guide one blindfolded person from their team towards a picture of a cow, and place a tail on the picture in the appropriate place. No talking is allowed and the only method of communication is by 'mooing'.

Give participants 2 minutes planning time, after which no talking is allowed.
Each team will have a different cow to aim for, and therefore you need to position each team accordingly so that they have a few obstacles to encounter.

Teams may struggle if they have not planned sufficiently or encounter communication problems that they may not have thought of, e.g. if their blindfolded person responds to another teams 'mooing'.

The winner is the team who gets the tail in the correct place in the quickest time.

Debrief

How did the staff feel not knowing where they were going? Link this into work as staff have to trust the leaders (managers / supervisors / leadership team etc.) even though they may not know what the end result will be in a task.

Did the team work together to decide who would do what?

Did they practice - i.e. make good use of time?

How was the person chosen to be blindfolded?

Did they have fun?

6. Scrambled Cities

1. IARSP ....

2. EWN KORY ....

3. SCWOOM ....

4. SOL SEELGNA ....

5. GACOHIC ....

6. RACEBLOAN ....

7. RUMHAD ....

8. DOONNL ....

9. HET TANCAIV ....

10. NAILM ....

11. THERP ....

12. ROKY ....

13. DRAIDM ....

14. MORE ....

15. DENYYS ....

16. TOOKY ....

17. NOAHPEENGC ....

18. BOREMENUL ....

19. NANIEV ....

20. BIDLUN ....

Running The Exercise

Distribute copies of the scrambled cities quiz to each participant.

Each item can be unscrambled to identify a city.

Answers are as follows:

1. Paris
2. New York
3. Moscow
4. Los Angeles
5. Chicago
6. Barcelona
7. Durham
8. London
9. The Vatican
10. Milan
11. Perth
12. York
13. Madrid
14. Rome
15. Sydney
16. Tokyo
17. Copenhagen
18. Melbourne
19. Vienna
20. Dublin

7. Picture Quiz

Requirements
Sheet with pictures of famous celebrities.

Running The Exercise
Hand out copies of the Celebrity sheet advising participants to identify each of the celebrities in the pictures.

8. Decipher the hidden meaning of each picture / set of words

Hand out copies of the brainteaser advising participants that each block represents a celebrity or a well know phrase or saying.

Answers can be found on the page following the question sheet.

1.	2.	3.	4.
I Q FGH JKLMNOP RST	**PLASMA** H2O	NOXQQ1VIT	arrest you're
5.	6.	7.	8.
P NOANO Y	cy cy	B ILL ED	POLMOMICE
9.	10.	11.	12.
⭕ **ME**	*That*	**CAR JACK TON**	111111 another another another another another another
13.	14.	15.	16.
ME ME ME AL AL AL day	HAMLET WORDS	CA SE CASE	⭕ ⭕ moving ⭕ moving

Answers:

1. I　　　Q FGH JKLMNOP　RST (High IQ)	2. **PLASMA** H2O (Blood Is Thicker Than Water)	3. NOXQQ1VIT (No Excuse For It)	4. arrest you're (You're Under Arrest)
5. 　　　P 　NOANO 　　　Y (Pay Through The Nose)	6. cy　　　cy (Cyclones)	7. B　ILL　ED (Sick In Bed)	8. POLMOMICE (Mother In Law)
9. **ME** (This Rounds On Me)	10. *That* (Fancy That)	11. **CAR　　JACK** **TON** (Jack In The Box)	12. 111111 another another another another another another (6 Of One Half A Dozen of Another)
13. ME　ME　ME AL　　AL　　AL day (3 Square Meals A Day)	14. HAMLET WORDS (Play On Words)	15. CA　　SE 　　CASE (Open And Shut Case)	16. (Moving In the Right Circles)

9. Brain Teaser

1	2	3	4
YYY MEN	VAD ERS	SAILING CCCCCCC	The Weather Feeling

5	6	7	8
BEND DRAW DRAW DRAW	LE VEL	DIAL	YOUNG YOUNG DRINK DRINK

9	10	11	12
TEKCIT	SYMPHON	GSEG	PING WILLOW

13	14	15	16
BRING EFIL EFIL	HISTORY HISTORY HISTORY	OU T C R	B AE DUMR

17	18	19	20
DNA 4TH	POLMUMICE	M CE M CE M CE	AT THE • OF ON

Answers:

1	2	3	4
YYY MEN	VAD ERS	SAILING CCCCCCC	The Weather Feeling
(three wise men)	(space Invaders)	(Sailing on the Seven seas)	(Feeling under the weather)

5	6	7	8
BEND DRAW DRAW DRAW	LE VEL	DIAL	YOUNG YOUNG DRINK DRINK
(Bend over Backwards)	(split Level)	(Laid back)	(Too young to drink)

9	10	11	12
TEKCIT	SYMPHON	GSEG	PING WILLOW
(Return ticket)	(Unfinished Symphony)	(Scrambled Eggs)	(Weeping Willow)

13	14	15	16
BRING EFIL EFIL	HISTORY HISTORY HISTORY	OU T C R	B AE DUMR
(Bring back To life)	(History repeating itself)	(Out of court)	(Bermuda Triangle)

17	18	19	20
DNA 4TH	POLMUMICE	M CE M CE M CE	AT THE • OF ON
(Back and forth)	(Mother-in- Law)	(Three blind mice)	(At the point of no return)

10. Hidden Squares

Requirements
Copy of the figure on the attached sheet for each participant

Running The Exercise
Provide each participant with the attached handout and ask them to quickly count the total number of squares seen, and advise the number orally.

The correct answer is 30, developed as follows:
1 whole square
16 individual squares
9 squares of four units each
4 squares of nine units each

11. <u>The Strange Addition</u>

Write the following sum on the flipchart:

5 + 5 + 5 = 550

(Make sure you make the pluses large!)

Now ask your delegates to make this sum correct by using only one line.

SOLUTION

You do it like this:

5 + 545 = 550

The second plus sign (+) becomes a 4!!

Exercises

1. Action Planning:

Split the participants into 2 groups. Ask each group to create a list of 10 "must do's" regarding the subject;

E.g   build rapport
        Issue brochure
        Offer examples to customer
        Handle objections
        Give features and benefits
        Ask valuable building questions etc

Bring the groups back and compare lists. Agree a definitive list of 10 "must do" actions.

2. Advert

Ask the Participants to design an advert regarding the subject

3. Website

Ask the Participants to design website regarding the subject

4. Pro's and Con's

Split the participants into groups. Create lists of pros and cons, good and bad…

5. Folding arms

Ask the participants to fold their arms across their chests.

Next, ask them to try to quickly reverse the position. It is surprisingly difficult. Where one-way feels comfortable, the other feels completely wrong. Evidence suggests that this may well be a genetic gesture that cannot be changed.

Use this to demonstrate the difficulty some people have when changing, emphasised the desire to go back to what feels "normal"

Quotations

The use of appropriate and inspirational quotations is hugely motivational.

The application of Inspirational quotations, phrases and sayings within training and development activities evokes a hugely motivational response. They contribute to motivation as they provide positive examples and role modelling. Visualisation is a powerful motivational tool. Quotations offer inspirational words which stimulate motivational images and feelings for the brain to visualise.

The positive imagery which exists in these inspirational words is genuinely motivational for people.

When using quotes to stimulate motivation and to open the mind to new ideas and concepts it is important to choose material that is both relevant and appropriate.

Motivational posters illustrating inspirational quotes can be posted around the training room. They can be added to handouts, PowerPoint presentations or be presented on the flip-chart.

Following are some examples of inspirational words and phrases which can be used to illicit these responses:

Whether you think you can all you think you can't you're right.
Henry Ford

You'll never leave where you are, until you decide where you'd rather be.
Robert Brockman

Everything is obvious once it has been pointed out.
Jimmy Miller

You gotta have goals!
Zig Ziglar

Take pride in how far you have come and have faith in how far you can go.
Christian Larson

Life takes on meaning when you become motivated, set goals and charge after them in an unstoppable manner.
Les Brown

One hundred percent of the shots you don't take don't go in.
Wayne Gretzky

Many highly intelligent people are poor thinkers. Many people of average intelligence are skilled thinkers. The power of a car is separate from the way a car is driven.
Edward de Bono

It is never too late to be what you might have been.
George Elliot

Some think of what is and ask why. I think of what isn't and ask why not?
Robert Kennedy

Be the change you wish to see in the world.
Mahatma Gandhi

You've got to be before you can do, and you've got to do before you can have.
Zig Ziglar

The most important thing in life is not to capitalise on your successes - any fool can do that. The really important thing is to profit from your mistakes.
William Bolitho

People who regard themselves as highly efficacious act, think, and feel differently from those who perceive themselves as inefficacious. They produce their own future, rather than simply foretell it.
Albert Bandura

Why not go out on a limb? That's where the fruit is.
Will Rogers

Most people never run far enough on their first wind to find out they've got a second. Give your dreams all you've got and you'll be amazed at the energy that comes out of you.
William James

No-one ever listened themselves out of a job.
Calvin Coolidge

There is none so blind as those who will not listen.
William Slater

Words are, of course, the most powerful drug used by mankind.
Rudyard Kipling

I not only use all the brains I have, but all I can borrow.
Woodrow Wilson

Better go home and make a net, rather than dive for fish at random.
Chinese proverb

Genius is one percent inspiration, ninety-nine percent perspiration.
Thomas Alva Edison

I have learned that success is to be measured not so much by the position that one has reached in life as by the obstacles overcome while trying to succeed.
Booker T Washington

Understanding human needs is half the job of meeting them.
Adlai Stevenson

If you want to change what you get, you need to change what you do
Jimmy Miller

A person who graduated yesterday and stops studying today is uneducated tomorrow.
Unknown

Common sense is not always common practice.
Unknown

No matter how thin you slice it, there is always two sides!
Unknown

A mistake is only a mistake if you don't learn from it.
Unknown

Catch a man a fish feed him for a day. Teach him how to fish and feed him for life.
Unknown

The cream always rises to the top.
Unknown

Amateurs practise until they get it right. Professionals practise until they cannot get it wrong.
Unknown

The Stone Age didn't end because they ran out of stones.
Unknown

Summary

The way in which a training course or programme is delivered has a significant effect on its ultimate success.

Whether it is setting up the course, creating the right environment or gaining and maintaining the participation of those attending, the application of simple yet effective techniques will contribute greatly to the experience of the learners and therefore the ultimate success of the training and subsequently the trainer.

Being able to remember names is a valuable skill, the impact of which can prove extraordinary. It is an effective rapport building technique which makes an incredibly good impression on everyone.

Mind Accessing or the ability to open minds to new ideas and concepts involves breaking down mental barriers helping us engage our respective audiences.

Mind Accessing techniques can be used to Gain Attention, Maintain Interest, Create Desire, Reinforce your information and message or Offer reassurance, forming an invaluable training resource. It should be something which is constantly applied and used in all aspects of training design and delivery.

Whilst rewarding, learning can prove draining. The use of exercises and energisers will help the learner maintaining focus, attention and concentration throughout the course.

References

ALLIGER, G. and JANAK, E. (1989) Kirkpatrick's levels of training criteria: thirty years later. *Personnel Psychology.*

Bandura, A. (1977) *Social Learning Theory*, Englewood Cliffs, NJ: Prentice Hall.

Bee, R and Bee, F. (1994) *Training Needs Analysis and Evaluation.* London, Institute of Personnel and Development

BRAMLEY, P. (1996). *Evaluating tra*ining. London: Chartered Institute of Personnel and Development.

Bruner, J. (1960, 1977) *The Process of Education*, Cambridge Ma.: Harvard University Press.

BURGOYNE, J. (1973). An action research experiment in the evaluation of a management course. *Journal of Management Studies.,*

CRONBACH, L. (1963). Evaluation for course improvement. In: HEATH, R. (ed). *New curricula.* New York: Harper & Row.

EASTERBY-SMITH, M. (1994) *Evaluating management development, training and education.* Aldershot: Gower.

Fontana, (1988) *Psychology for Teachers*, British psychological Society/Macmillan, Basingstoke

Gagné, R. M. (1985) *The Conditions of Learning* 4e, New York: Holt, Rinehart and Winston.

Gardner, H. (1993) *Intelligence Reframed. Multiple intelligences for the 21st century,* New York: Basic Books.

GUBA, E. and LINCOLN, Y. (1989) *Fourth generation evaluation.* London: Sage.

HAMBLIN, A. (1974). *Evaluation and control of training.* Maidenhead: McGraw-Hill.

Hartley, J. (1998) *Learning and Studying. A research perspective,* London: Routledge.

Honey, P and Mumford, A. (1992) A *Manual of Learning Styles.* Maidenhead, Honey.

Honey, P and Mumford, A. (1992) *Managing Your Learning Environment.* Maidenhead, Honey.

Kolb, D. A. (1984) *Experiential Learning,* Englewood Cliffs, NJ.: Prentice Hall.

LATHAM, G. and SAARI, L. (1979) The application of social learning theory to training supervisors through behavioural modelling. *Journal of Applied Psychology.*

Marchington, M and Wilkinson, A. (1996) *Core Personnel and Development.*
London, Institute of Personnel and Development

MATHIEU, J. and LEONARD, R. (1987) Applying utility concepts to a training program in supervisory skills: a time-based approach. *Journal of Academic Management*. Vol 30, No 2. pp316-335.

Hergenhahn, B. R. and Olson, M. H. (1997) *An Introduction to Theories of Learning* 5e, Upper Saddle River, NJ: Prentice-Hall.

Lave, J. and Wenger, E. (1991) *Situated Learning. Legitimate peripheral participation*, Cambridge: University of Cambridge Press.

Maslow, A. (1968) *Towards a Psychology of Being* 2e, New York: Van Nostrand.

Maslow, A. (1970) *Motivation and Personality* 2e, New York: Harper and Row.

Merriam, S. and Caffarella (1991, 1998) *Learning in Adulthood. A comprehensive guide*, San Francisco: Jossey-Bass.

PATON, M. (1986). *Utilisation-focused evaluation*. Beverly Hills: Sage.

Piaget, J. (1926) *The Child's Conception of the World*, London: Routledge and Kegan

H. E. Gruber and J. J. Voneche (1977) *The Essential Piaget: an interpretative reference and guide*, London: Kogan

M. A. Boden's (1979) *Piaget*, London: Fontana

Skinner, B. F. (1973) *Beyond Freedom and Dignity*, London: Penguin.

Smith, M. K. (1999) 'The cognitive orientation to learning', *the encyclopaedia of informal education,*

Tennant, M. (1988, 1997) *Psychology and Adult Learning,* London: Routledge.

Tennant, M. and Pogson, P. (1995) *Learning and Change in the Adult Years. A developmental perspective,* San Francisco: Jossey-Bass.

Rogers, C. and Freiberg, H. J. (1993) *Freedom to Learn* (3rd edn.), New York: Merrill.

H. Kirschenbaum and V. L. Henderson (eds.) (1990) *The Carl Rogers Reader,* London: Constable.

Printed in Poland
by Amazon Fulfillment
Poland Sp. z o.o., Wrocław